Praise for Sarah Robbins

"Sarah Robbins is an incredible generation Y leader who at her young age has accomplished more than most of us would dream possible. Already a stellar speaker and trainer, she continues to grow herself and her business through hard work, passion, and dedication to her team. Seeing her dynamism and determination today, we can only imagine who she will be and what she will achieve ten, twenty, and thirty years from now."

—Chris and Josephine M. Gross, Ph.D.
Founders, *Networking Times*

"I have read more than 500 books in my twenty-seven year career in this profession, and only a handful have ever made me say, 'Wow!' This book is a life-changing GIFT to our profession! Sarah shares her gift for this profession brilliantly, step-by-step, and this is a MUST READ for anyone who owns a home business! Get one for you and for each person on your team—now and as they join!"

—Doug Firebaugh
Passionfire International

"The world is changed by our example, not by our opinion, and this is where Sarah Robbins sizzles! Her heart to help others, her humility to constantly learn and become better, her courage to do so with class, respect, and honor... Sarah leads by her example, and in leadership, that matters most."

—Art Jonak
Founder, The Mastermind Event (MM)

"Sarah has an incredible passion, spirit, and energy for the network marketing profession. She has the ability to communicate in a way that is not a 'preachy' lecture, nor does she coddle—she is a master of influence so that when you listen to her ideas, you feel more capable as well as inspired to achieve everything you want."

—Andrea Waltz
Co-Author, *Go for No!*

"Network marketing is a simple business, really. All you will ever do is learn how to do something, get good at it, and then teach your people how to do what you do. From your very first day all the way to the very top level of income and achievement, that's what you'll do. So it makes great sense to learn what to do from the best. Sarah Robbins is one of the greatest networkers in the world. I admire her tremendously. You will not learn from better."

—John Milton Fogg
Author, *The Greatest Networkers in the World*

"Sarah Robbins is one of the most passionate, purpose-filled leaders I know. Her inspirational story is a blessing to this profession. Sarah leads with heart, vision, humility, and integrity."

—Donna Valdes
Cofounder, Real Savvy Success

"As one of the top network marketing professionals in the world today, Sarah is the real deal. She runs a flourishing multi-million-dollar direct sales business of her own and teaches others how to achieve their own success. Her training includes both high level strategies and day-to-day tactics that apply to any direct selling organization."

—Melissa Lynch
National Program Director

ROCK YOUR NETWORK MARKETING BUSINESS

How to Become a
Network Marketing ROCK STAR

SARAH ROBBINS

For information on quantity discounts, please write to:
Sarah Robbins
43311 Joy Rd., #119
Canton, MI 48187-2075 USA

Published by:
Rockin' Robbins Publishing
43311 Joy Rd., #119
Canton, MI 48187-2075 USA

Book Production Services Provided by:
Prime Concepts Group
www.PrimeConcepts.com

About SarahRobbins.com

SarahRobbins.com is a FREE resource dedicated to helping educate, enlighten, enrich, and elevate the entire network marketing profession. You can find free training, videos, and blogs at **www.SarahRobbins.com**.

We welcome you to enjoy and participate in our Facebook community: **www.Facebook.com/sarahrobbinsfanpage**

It would be an honor if you would take a few moments to write a rockin' review of this book on Amazon.

BULK DISCOUNT PROGRAM:
Our goal is to get this book into the hands of your rock stars, as well as up-and-coming rock stars that join your team. To make this goal a reality, we have included a bulk discount program that will allow your leaders to have this book on hand at all times. We encourage you to:

- Gift a copy to every person who joins your team.
- Gift a copy to everyone who is on your team.
- Make copies available at each meeting or event. The more you empower, the higher you elevate!

1-9	$12 each	100-499	$6 each
10-24	$10 each	500-999	$5 each
25-49	$8 each	1,000	$4 each
50-99	$7 each		

To order, visit www.SarahRobbins.com/store

ACKNOWLEDGEMENTS

I'm not a professional writer. I'm a formerly shy teacher who found network marketing, and it radically changed my life. As a former educator, I have a passion for sharing my learning to help others achieve the success they've dreamed of through network marketing. I've been gifted with much wisdom from my mentors over the past five years, and sincerely believe a gift isn't a gift until you give it away. So here I am today, ready to share this gift with all of you—holding nothing back.

I ask you to be forgiving of my writing imperfections as you read and instead notice the passion and content on the page. Terminology may vary (customer, product vs. services, consultants, distributors), but the core message is the same for many.

It is my hope you can take some of what you learn, implement it into your current company's system, and use it to completely rock your network marketing business.

Before we get started, I want to thank some VIP people in my life:

God, I thank you for the wisdom you've granted me, the people you've placed in my path, and the provision you've provided that allows us to bless others.

To my husband Phil, you are God's greatest gift to me on this earth. Thank you for your wisdom, patience, prayers, kindness, and complete support on this journey. You gifted your business to support me in this endeavor. I am forever grateful.

To my mother Kris, thank you for saying "yes" and encouraging me to take the chance that would change my life! You are an amazing mother, leader, role model, and friend. You brought me into this world and into the network marketing world! I am forever grateful.

To my family, you are my everything. You are my support system, prayer partners, and very best friends. I couldn't ask for better parents, siblings, and extended family.

To my mentors (of whom there are many and you know who you are), thank you for your wisdom and sowing into my life. I hope to bless others as much as you've blessed me and be a good steward of the gifts you've given me, using them to empower, equip, and educate the next generation of network marketing leaders. And a special shout-out to Chris and Josephine Gross of *Networking Times* who have provided a professional publication, and incredible opportunities and stories to all of us!

To my spiritual "parents" Doug and Jodi Firebaugh, thank you for sowing seeds of greatness in our life. You've modeled to us that true success comes from God!

To my corporate "dream team," thank you for providing us a vehicle and the resources that are changing many lives! We appreciate your hard work!

To my "rock stars" of Team Rockin' Robbins, we adore you! Without you, our success and this book would not exist! We are forever grateful for your dedication, hard work, and leadership! I love you and honor you! Now a special shout-out to my "top ten personal team leaders" at the time I write this book (I know many more are to come)! Natalia Yosco, Stephanie Goetz, Amy Dagan, Emily Piniatoglou, Stacey Coler-Dark, Susie Sheftel, Prudy Ferrone, Marie Machesko, Jeannine O'Leary, and Nikki Lazo are all mentioned in this book! You are my power partners and some of my best friends!

To all of *you*, thank you for believing in us, in the power of our profession, and more importantly, for believing in the power of your dream! Rock on, rock stars!

TABLE OF CONTENTS

CHAPTER 1

Demystifying the Big Build

Hey there, rock stars! Sarah "Rockin'" Robbins here. Welcome to the Rock Star Recruiting School. This book will teach you the system that helped me achieve seven-figure success, as well as many members of my team who have their own six-or-seven-figure success stories. Six-and-seven-figure success certainly didn't happen overnight. It wasn't easy; it was certainly worth it. Here's my story:

I'm a formerly shy teacher by trade, who was living in one of the more depressed economies in the country. I had just moved, married, and began my brand-new job teaching kindergarten. I was in my twenties. While I loved teaching, we were facing financial difficulties, paying bills with change. I was also facing the loss of my job and our first home. This caused me to look for extra income, and my search led me to network marketing.

I first found my company when it was a top-selling clinical brand in high-end department stores. I began freelancing for the brand to supplement my teaching salary. During this time, our founders were looking for ways they could leverage their brand and bring it to the masses in today's social economy. Because everyone is online, they decided to choose a social selling model and make a transition from retail to networking marketing. They asked me to join them, along with my mother Kris, and we said yes!

Because we were the first to join, we didn't have training or marketing materials. In fact, we didn't even have a compensation plan yet! All we had was our belief; we believed so strongly in the opportunity we were offering and the product we were promoting. From the outside looking in, it may not have appeared that we would have a very high "survival rate," but today my mother and I are both seven-figure income earners within our company.

Through our persistence and commitment to personal and professional growth, we were able to establish a system and help others get off to a great start. I was able to retire from teaching so I could pursue my dream of starting a foundation for children. In four years, by the age of twenty-nine, I became our company's first six-figure *monthly* earner, and we've since mentored many six-and-seven-figure annual earners on our team. Many have earned free company cars and are enjoying luxury trips to fabulous destinations around the world!

I'm proud of what our profession has done for people! My greatest joy is what we are able to *give*. We offer hope and freedom to those who join us in this incredible business model, and we also give hope to those outside our opportunity as we are now able to bless them with our time, talent, and resources.

Success in network marketing didn't come easy for me. I wasn't a fast starter, and I failed forward quite a bit. But the most important thing was that I didn't quit, and I learned a lot.

Failing Forward

I recently had coffee with one of my mentors and friends, Leslie, who reminded me of my early days when I used to be one of the lowest earning leaders within the company. Leslie reminded me of the time she and I went out to an Italian restaurant after an event. She recalled, "I remember you crying over your pasta, wondering how you were ever going to make $3,000 per month in network marketing, and here you are today making six-figures per month! Sarah, when people ask me how you did it, I simply say one thing: 'She was coachable.'" Leslie was right!

When I started my business, success didn't come easy for me. I had many challenges some may view as hurdles, even from the starting gates: I was young, broke, most of my network was young and broke, and I was shy. In fact, I remember approaching someone for the first time about my products at a cosmetic counter. My hands were shaking, my knees were knocking, and I literally saw stars! I remember doing the "network marketing verbal vomit" all over her. She just stared at me like a deer in headlights.

I was so embarrassed! I ran out to my car, cried, and called my mom. When I asked my mom if I should go back, she said, "No, don't go back there. Get out of there!" So I put the pedal to the metal, and cried the whole way home. I wondered how I would ever be able to succeed in the business of networking if I was afraid to talk to people.

Yet, I didn't want to give up. I needed to earn extra money in case I lost my teaching job due to school budget cuts. Although I was shy, I was coachable—I was willing to learn and plug into a proven system. I was committed—I wasn't going to give up until I surpassed my teaching income!

When I started my business, my only desire was to earn an extra $3,000 per month in case I lost my teaching job. My mom and I were the first consultants in the company, so we had no upline leading and guiding us. Having been a product educator formerly for our company, I did what I knew how to do: I started selling a lot of product! I was earning a few hundred to a thousand dollars residual income each month. As people reordered products, the money kept coming in for effort I put forth previously. This was great considering I only had very part-time hours to put into my business.

My mom (who's my upline) loved it because she was making a great residual income from my sales, too! We felt like we were on to something, and that this business opportunity was our best kept secret! So one day, my mom called me and said, "Sarah, this opportunity is so huge! Let's not tell anyone! Let's keep this our own little secret!" (We didn't have a fully executed compensation plan at the time, so we figured we would just continue to sell.) How many of you know, in a business of networking, that's the last thing you want to do? But being a good daughter I said, "Okay!" and committed to just continue selling products!

Now of course, that didn't last long. We eventually "saw the light" through reading books about our profession. We became students of the profession. I read many stories of top earners in our profession; I quickly learned that all of the six -and-seven-figure earners leveraged their time and increased their income by building a team—one simple shift. When I made the shift from product sales to power prospecting for the business, I watched my check go from a few thousand dollars to more than $10,000 per month in just a few months. That's the power of prospecting.

Finding Success Through Prospecting

What is prospecting? Different dictionary versions define it as "looking for gold." Prospecting is the process of talking to people in hopes that you will find some who are interested in joining you in promoting your products or services, or in joining your business. In the process of these conversations, you'll "sift through" a lot of people to find a few who will join you. Then you'll have a lot of people join you, of who will work at varying paces. Keep in mind, it only takes a few "power partners" to change your life! That's your "gold!" Remember, you may have to talk to a lot to find those few, much like sifting for gold. If I told you that you had three gold bricks in your backyard, would you continue to dig until you found them? I would!

I'm living proof of this concept. I've been sifting for a long time. I've probably talked to thousands of people since I started my business more than five years ago. I've had more than one hundred people join me as business partners. Of those, I have about thirty people still working our business at a moderate pace. Of those, I have ten top leaders in our pay plan at this time. Of those, about three people account for a good majority of my income.

What happened to the rest? As a teacher, I pride myself on education, but I quickly realized you can't motivate people who are unwilling to do what it takes to succeed. They need to want it for themselves more than you want it for them. I can't take credit for peoples' success or failure. I am only responsible to get them off to a great start. People will work at varying paces. Some people order product, some occasionally promote it, and some even enter into the "witness protection program"—they buy a kit and disappear! As you can see, there is power in working through the numbers. If you want to be successful in network marketing, you'll be sifting and sorting until you find your key leaders. You will never stop prospecting!

Is it a Numbers Game?

I've found the same stats and averages to be pretty similar industry-wide as they relate to how many you must personally talk to and sponsor before you strike gold. This observation was illustrated recently when I was invited on stage at a major event in our profession along with several top income earners. We all represented different products, and our companies had different pay plans. Some of us had a few years experience in the profession, some had decades of experience. We were each asked how many people we've personally sponsored in our business, and of those, how many account for 80 percent or more of our income. The answers were very similar.

We had all been in our business anywhere between 5-25 years. We each sponsored anywhere between 50-150 over time. Most of us had 80 percent of our income coming from anywhere between 1-3 legs, or leaders! I've seen this exercise done at many events in our profession since, and the results are pretty similar.

What does that mean? The major growth of your organization may be tied to just a few people, but you never know what your personal set off odds will be until after you succeed. You don't know how many conversations you'll have, or how many people will join you before you find "gold!" So get ready to talk it up! The more people you share with, the better your odds of finding your power partners!

The Cure to What Ails You in Your Business

The cure to what ails you in your business is your personal activity. Don't blame your progress or pace on your team. Take personal responsibility for your activity and respect their effort and pace. Never stop recruiting new customers and business partners. Focus on daily activity to progress toward success. My rule for myself is "five contacts per day keeps leads coming my way." If I'm home, I'm making five calls to people on my contact list. If I'm out, I am handing out five business cards and having conversations with people I meet. I'm not done until I've made those connections and continued to work through my numbers, which in turn, increase my odds for success.

What are Your Odds?

Your success is directly related to the degree to which you are willing to work to find others like yourself who are committed to succeeding. Would you be willing to hear many "nos" to sign up one hundred or more people until you "strike gold" and find three major producers like I did?

You have your own set of odds and you won't know what they are until after you've succeeded. If you haven't achieved the level of success you desire yet, you can give up and assume the business model doesn't work (but if you've seen success in your company, I assure you it does). Or you can accept the fact that you're working through your odds. Don't give up until you succeed!

Throughout this book, I will teach you my "success system" that has led many on my team to six-and-seven-figure success. It is my hope that as you implement these best practices, you can increase your confidence and sharpen your skills, which will improve your own set of odds! Are you ready to go for the gold?

Free Bonus!
Visit www.SarahRobbins.com/free-video/
to check out Sarah's video:
"Demystifying the Big Build"

CHAPTER 2

The Power of Our Profession

Welcome to the Rock Star Recruiting School!

This book will teach you my "Seven-Figure Success System." It's a simple system that's helped me to build a big business. Remember, there's not one magic bullet that leads to six-or-seven-figure success; success in network marketing comes from doing a number of little things right. This system will teach you how to develop an entrepreneur's mindset, build bigger volume with a large customer and distributor base, and establish simple systems that will lead to dynamic duplication for your team—and more!

This book will bring you "back to school with Sarah." I am going to teach you all that I've learned over the past five years of reading, studying, being mentored, and mentoring others to achieve million-dollar success. If you are coachable and stay committed to your business, you will grow, and so will your business. Are you coachable? Are you committed? Are you promoting this book to your team? It's essential that you learn these success principles together and implement them as a group for greater results.

Whatever You're Dreaming, Dream Bigger

I want to first start by helping you build your belief in the profession.

19

I believe that network marketing is one of the smartest business models on the planet! It is a model that takes ordinary people like me and helps them to achieve extraordinary results! Where else could a formerly shy teacher in her twenties compress a 30-50 year career into 3-5 years and elevate to success that others only dream of, and most people can't even conceive! I've fallen head over heels in love with our profession, and if I had to recreate my wealth all over again, I'd do it in network marketing!

Here are a few reasons why I am in love with this profession:

This is a brilliant business model where instead of investing in advertising and celebrity endorsement, companies invest in our success. It allows us to leverage the integrity of big brands and the time, talent, and resources of major corporations. Startup costs are low. It's a simple business model that doesn't require a college degree, overhead, employees, or a brick and mortar shop. It's a scalable business, and it's just plain smart. The Direct Selling Association recently celebrated its 100-year anniversary, so it's a tried and true business model that's proven to be solid. Network marketing is not going anywhere.

Network marketing provides a turnkey business where you start at a low cost, it carries little to no risk, and there's no experience necessary to begin. It carries many incredible benefits, such as: freedom and flexibility, financial opportunity, fun and friendship, and fabulous opportunities for growth! Let's talk about these!

1. Freedom and Flexibility
In network marketing, you don't trade hours for dollars, or your time for someone else's money. You can work

your business part-time, any time! There's no commute to work. You create your hours, block out the important things in your life, and plan around them. Essentially, you design a professional life that fits around the rest of your life. Often started as a plan B, it can easily become a plan A. I started my business to supplement my teacher's salary, and I was able to generate wealth beyond my wildest dreams!

Many people are surviving within multi-income households, losing valuable time with their family. Others are looking for extra earning potential due to the current economic climate. The network marketing profession can provide an incredible alternative for those looking to supplement their income around the commitments of their family. You don't have to go back to school or take on another full-time job. Network marketing allows you to choose a dream life over a dream job! All the while, you can be fully present in your family's life.

2. Financial Opportunity

Network marketing is one of the best choices if you're looking to create unlimited earning potential but have little upfront money. We leverage our upfront investment and have the opportunity for an exponential ROI. Network marketing allows you to create passive residual income and get paid over and over again for work you began upfront.

If you give your business enough time and effort, you are able to compress a 30-50 year career into 3-5 years!

Your business can lead to ongoing residual income for you. If you build it right, you can get paid on the royalties or residual income forevermore! Our business model provides true leverage, which gives you security. Wealth is created through leverage. It is an incredible financial vehicle that allows you to pursue all of your life's goals and dreams.

In network marketing, we also turn expenses into an income while buying from our own product store. You can share your success with your product or service with others. This allows you to make money or save money. You will get paid to talk about your transformative products or services and our award-winning business model. You get paid to talk about what you love, and you can earn amazing bonuses, competitive commissions, and incredible incentives! This is the company's way of rewarding you for a job well done. In network marketing, you don't just get paid, you also get recognized!

3. Fun and Friendship
In our business model, you choose those you partner with in business. You have the chance to build your success, all while helping others to succeed! You celebrate your success together in countless trips and trainings around the world! One of the greatest rewards of building my business has been the friendships I've developed.

4. Fabulous Opportunities for Personal and Professional Growth
You are in business for yourself—not by yourself. In our business model, you receive incredible training through

your company and team training systems that are provided. You also receive incredible personal development opportunities so you can grow as a person, which helps to support you inside and outside our business model. This leads to incredible life and leadership skills. You grow in confidence and communication! What is the best part of all? You earn as you learn! The personal and professional growth opportunities definitely outweigh the paycheck for me!

To sum it up all up in one word, network marketing provides *freedom!*

Give this Time to Grow

Throughout this book I will share "how to" make this work for you, but first I want to get you set up with proper expectations.

I want you to have realistic expectations of what it will take, as well as how long it could take to be successful in your business. Success doesn't magically happen overnight. I want you to think as anyone would who was considering embarking on any new career. Starting any new career or business, you know there will be a learning curve of both personal and professional growth. You know there will be an output of time and sometimes resources. You understand it will take time to develop proficiency. Some people go to school for their career. Developing a substantial story in network marketing is no different. Success in network marketing requires personal and professional growth. It takes time to develop your talent; I want you to commit to a minimum of five years in your business. Take the time to learn your company story and system, study this book, get good at sharing your story and your company's story, and give your business time to grow!

This business is a lot like rolling a snowball uphill. When you start, you're at the bottom of the hill with a tiny little snowball. As you share your business with more people who join you on the products or in your opportunity, the snowball slowly begins to grow. However, you sometimes feel like you're exerting all the effort as you are trekking uphill. Sometimes you feel like you're working full-time hours for less than minimum wage! This is because you haven't reached the top of the hill yet. If you keep going and you keep sharing, you will make it to the top. When you do, you can let that snowball soar down the other side. This is when you see momentum take place! It rolls faster and faster downhill, collecting its own snow. This is when duplication happens and you begin earning more money than you've ever dreamed in less time than most would think was possible.

Whatever you do, don't quit. You can make it to the top of the hill!

The Story of the $50 Million Woman

I want to share with you a story of why quitting should never cross your mind.

One of the top leaders on my team is a woman by the name of Susie. Susie learned about our business from someone she had worked with briefly. On December 31, she was introduced to me on a three-way call by her soon-to-be-sponsor, who at the time was my personal partner. Susie immediately caught the vision and enrolled on New Year's Eve—what a way to toast to new beginnings!

Unfortunately, Susie's sponsor got discouraged she had only enrolled one person. She decided the business wasn't for her, and she quit.

A few years later, her team of one (Susie) grew into an incredible team that spans across the entire country. In fact, it's one of the fastest growing teams in our company. Many team members are driving beautiful free cars, earning amazing incentive trips, and increasing their incomes. In fact, Susie was recently recognized as a "Million-Dollar Circle Achiever" at our company convention.

Can you imagine if Susie's sponsor stuck with the business? She started the business at about thirty years of age. After taxes and with conservative investments (not even taking into account organizational growth), she could have earned about $50 million over time if she hadn't walked away. For this reason, I've referred to her in industry events as the "$50 Million Woman."

One of my friends, Donna Johnson (another million-dollar earner), reminds me often: "Sarah, I know handfuls of people who would be millionaires today simply if they hadn't quit!" You never know what people will do or whom they will lead you to. Quitting is the surest way to fail!

I recently read that as many as 95 percent of those who remain in this industry for ten years or longer, working steadily at building their groups, reach their highest level of pay in their respective business.

If there's one thing that I know for sure about success is that it begins with a decision to be successful, a commitment to seeing it through, and you just can't quit. Early on, when we started our business with no training, no websites, and no mentoring, we made a decision to do whatever it takes! In my opinion, that is the greatest factor that leads to success—your decision. Whether you think you can or think you can't, you're right! So make a decision, be relentless, and be committed to do whatever it takes!

I am committed to your success! This book will provide the "how tos" for you—simple, systematic training that will empower you to become a higher achiever in our profession. It's up to you to implement what you learn; it's up to you to share this learning with your new distributors and team. It is my hope that you will gift a copy of this book to every leader and to every new distributor who joins your business in the future. Build their belief in your business, build their belief in our profession, and most importantly, build their belief in themselves! Get ready for a great journey of personal and professional growth! Let's rock this!

CHAPTER 3

Preparation: Think Like a CEO!

Welcome to the wonderful world of network marketing! What a powerful profession to be a part of! You are your own boss; you own your own business; you design your own future. You are the CEO of your own company! *Now what?*

The beauty of this profession is that it allows anyone, regardless of age or experience, to own their own company. This can be a challenge, too. Not everyone who joins is fully prepared to be a business owner. I've heard people say that the business should be kept so simple systematically that an eight-year-old can do it—we are just sharing and inviting. While I agree that we should keep things simple, people still struggle with limiting belief and a lack of self-motivation. Mindset and management of time and emotions are the places where people often get caught up. We have to develop an entrepreneurial mindset. In order to be successful, I want to talk to you about how to manage your expectations, your emotions, and your time. When you have total control over these areas, anything can be accomplished in your business!

Often we hear the saying, "Treat this like a business and it will pay like a business; treat this like a hobby and it will pay like a hobby!"

While most people start their business very part-time, it requires your full effort for you to be completely successful. Where does success begin in your business? It begins with you! So often we play the "blame game," sharing all the reasons why we weren't successful. Often times, the reason why we started (products, pay plan, partnership with our company or sponsor) is the very reason why we say the company didn't end up working. Funny, huh? It's easy to blame our upline or downline for our lack of success. But isn't this "independent business ownership"? The only name on your distributor account is yours. Yours is the only name on your paycheck! It's important for you to take action and own your success. Network marketing professionals take accountability for their actions, daily activity, and they own their results.

Developing Your Blueprint for Entrepreneurial Success

I started my business like most people, working very part-time alongside my full-time career and commitments. I was a brand-new teacher busy with lesson planning and preparation. I was actively involved in my church, my husband's business, and many of our volunteer projects. Like most, I was busy! I knew if I was to find success in my business, I had to implement systems and establish hours of operation in order to stay focused and make the most of the little time I did have available. I took everything day by day, telling myself, "I can do anything for a short period of time to produce long-term financial freedom for myself and my family!"

Many of you are probably facing a full-time schedule as well, whether it be due to your career, raising your family, or other countless commitments you face each day. It's critical that you learn how to make the most of your part-time hours so you can experience success in your business.

I've heard people say, "You can work your business part-time, but not some-time." What does that mean? It means that with the hours you do have to put into your business, you must be planned and purposeful; you must be prepared!

One of the first things most successful business owners do is establish hours of operation. Building a network marketing business is no different. It's important that you set aside a minimum of 10-15 hours of income-producing activity per week if you desire to duplicate a larger network. If you just want to sell retail products, you can get away with a bit less. Building a team requires more. You can't conduct events, calls, and trainings in just a few hours.

Busy work doesn't count toward your time. Busy work is comprised of checking Facebook, cleaning your office, calling your team to chat, or refreshing your sales reports over and over again to see what's happening in your business. Income-producing activity consists of a few things:

1. Sharing your business and inviting people to learn more.
2. Sharing your product or service and inviting people to try them.
3. Follow-up, signing people up, and getting them started.

Look at your weekly planner and block out your 10-15 hours per week now! You must control your time or your time controls you! We can't complain about our "busy schedule," as the only person who creates that schedule is *you*!

When setting aside your hours of operation, be sure to include time for: prospecting, presenting the opportunity over coffee and calls, attending or hosting local meetings and events, and getting educated at your team meetings and on team calls, too.

If you find yourself at all overwhelmed by your daily commitments, I encourage you to look at what can be cut out, such as: long phone conversations with friends, watching your favorite TV programs, and sitting on social media. You may have to learn to say "no" for a little while so you can say "yes" to the things you love—for the rest of your life!

I want you to even look at where you can outsource where it's inexpensive. When I was just starting my business, I hired a housecleaner to come every two weeks. Not only did it free me up from doing something I didn't love to do, it also gave me a whole extra afternoon to build my business for our future! Whatever you do, don't be swayed by daily distractions. If you are serious about your business, you will have to make some short-term "exchanges" to produce the long-term financial freedom and rewards that come with your business! You'll have to have laser-sharp focus, tunnel vision, and be like a dog with a bone—don't let go!

You have to be willing to pay a price for true time and financial freedom. Again, you'll find you have to consider where you can make short-term exchanges for long-term reward. We will talk about what to do during your income-producing activity time in the upcoming chapters. For now, I want to talk to you about another critical component to success in any business, and that's your personal and professional growth!

The Story of the Starving Baker

Have you heard the story about the starving baker?

Imagine: There is a brand-new, beautiful bakery built right down the road. The aroma of fresh pastries fills the air. This is where hot, delightful treats are served all day long. You go in. This baker is brilliant. You order your treat and watch as the baker does his thing! It is magnificent watching. He does everything himself. He cleans the tables, tends to the cash register, bakes the goods, and greets the guests. You start to notice that he's surprisingly thin. You begin to think, "He's so busy baking for others, he's forgetting to eat! He's starving himself."

Are you that starving baker? Most of us are so busy that we fall into starving baker mode. We get so wrapped up in our jobs, our problems, the house, errands, and everyone else and their matters that we never push "pause" and take the time to feed ourselves. We feel hollow. Sometimes we feel fake. You are not fake; what you are is a starving baker. You've gotten busy and you've stopped growing. We've all been there before.

Taking time for our personal and professional growth provides nourishment for our souls, and it fuels our minds. It makes us more effective for everyone in our lives we influence—our families, friends, and our teams. If I could encourage all of you to implement one thing today, it would be to plan to wake up each day and just as you eat your breakfast to fuel your body, begin to feed your mind, too! You can only go as far as you grow!

I like to spend time each morning devoting attention to my personal and professional growth. It's the perfect way to power-start my day and to prepare myself for new opportunities! I like to end each day the same way, so I am thinking and believing positive things before my head hits the pillow. Therefore, I don't start or end my day with chaos, emails, TV, text messages, etc. I feed and fuel myself with prayer, devotions, reading personal and professional development materials, and listening to positive and uplifting music. I even fill in the "empty time" when I drive listening to training CDs, making my car a "rolling university." I listen to things that teach me how to become a better person and more effective leader. I am extremely intentional about my daily self-programming so I am more effective as a wife, friend, sister, daughter, and leader. I realize that my business can only grow as much as I do.

My "Come to the Parking Lot!" Moment

I'll be the first to admit, I wasn't always a positive person. When I first started my business, like most people, I was a "big bundle of doubt and fear." I would allow every distraction to discourage, and allow every disappointment to de-motivate me. I had my daily "I quit" moments. If you, too, are on the (insert your company name here) roller coaster, it's time to stop the ride, refocus, recommit, re-establish your goals, and re-start.

I used to say things like: "Nobody is joining my team," or "Everyone is quitting." Wouldn't you know? That's exactly what was happening! Through personal development, I learned that your words are seeds. Words are capable of bringing a harvest in your life—good or bad. My words were either going to be fertilizer to my growing dream, or they would poison it. Personal development took me on a two-year journey into a deep discovery about the power of my thoughts and words. One of the critical moments in time on this personal growth journey happened during what I call my "Come to the parking lot!" moment.

One day I was sitting in a parking lot in my car, waiting for my meeting to start. I got a call from one of my mom's friends, Rachel, who is also a leader in our company. At the time, I was struggling in my business. I picked up the phone, and she immediately opened with, "Sarah, do you want to know what's been holding you back?" I was so excited! She was finally going to give me the "magic bullet" to success! She proceeded, "You are doing all the right things by going through the motions, showing up to every meeting and call. Your problem is that your thoughts toward your business and team don't align with your goals for success. Your words aren't aligning either. You need to make a decision to be successful." That was one of the most honest conversations anyone has had with me, and to be honest, it was a defining moment in my life. She was right—I was going through the motions, but I hadn't really made up in my mind and declared I was going to be successful!

That was the day I made up my mind and began to change my daily declarations, saying: "I have the fastest growing team in the company!" "I will be a top leader and earner!" At the time, it wasn't true, but these daily affirmations, when spoken out loud, elevated my belief, which changed my confidence, ultimately affected my odds, and created results. Today, those declarations are true; I became the top earner in my company! How did I go from being a shy teacher in my twenties, and one of the lowest earning leaders, to eventually becoming the top earner? Not because I worked harder on my business. The truth be told, I worked harder on my personal growth than I did my business during that time. I believe a large portion of my success was due to the fact that I spent two whole years studying the power of my words, and I was intentional about my thoughts and declarations! That's the power of personal development!

As you prepare to become an empowered entrepreneur, I want to ask you: What are your attitudes about success? What are you saying about yourself or your team daily? What are you thinking? Your thoughts become your words; your words become your actions; your actions determine your outcome! Much of our success boils down to our belief—in our company, in our profession, and of course in ourselves. This is why daily personal and professional development is the key! Invest in yourself; invest in your team's dream; speak life into them; and increase their self-esteem by teaching personal development as much as you teach the professional development skills.

I love the story of A.L. Williams in the book *Pushing People Up*. He was a high school coach who had a dream to create unlimited opportunity and to help ordinary people achieve extraordinary things. He took a bunch of teachers and coaches and created a network marketing company that sold life insurance. By the seventh year, they sold more term life insurance than New York Life, Metropolitan, and Prudential combined, which were more than a century old. How? He did it through boosting up peoples' self-confidence. This illustrates personal development at its finest!

Ask yourself, "What type of culture do I want to create on my team?" Culture begins with you, and it starts today! Your words and your actions will duplicate down to your team, and a leader is only as good as his or her team. Grow yourself, and your team will grow! Be the leader they're looking for!

True leaders can cast a vision and they know where they are going. How do they know where they are going? They plan for it and they communicate it to their team. What are your plans for you and your team? Where do you want to take them? Have you shared your vision with them?

Making Your Dream a Reality

One of the most important exercises you can do as you begin your business is to identify your "reason why." What is driving you emotionally to develop a successful business? Your "why" is your long-term vision for success in your business. How can you know the route to take if you don't know where you're going? How can you bring others with you?

Let me ask you a few questions: If time and money were no issue, how would your life look? Where would you live? What would you drive? What would you do with your time? Would you have any debt? In other words, what will a successful business do for your life, your family's life, and your lifestyle?

I want you to clearly write down why you are doing your business. The more specific, the more powerful it will be! Make it compelling so it causes you to find the time, face your fears, and persevere!

Is your reason "why" to have a college fund for your children, to pay off debt, buy your dream home, become more self-reliant, or are you funding your retirement? For me, I wanted to start a foundation for women and children that I would fund through my business.

One of the first things I did when I started my network marketing business was create my reason "why." I remember working with one of my mentors who asked me, "Sarah, what's your reason 'why'?"

I told her, "I want to start a foundation for children that is fully funded through my network marketing business. It will provide housing, teaching and training for mothers, and a camp for kids!"

Impressed, she asked, "And how much will that cost?"

"Millions," I told her.

She proceeded to ask: "And how does that feel?"

"I have to admit, it's overwhelming," I said.

You see, my "why" was so big that at times, instead of serving as a motivator, it would de-motivate me. I was so overwhelmed by my dream that I often felt defeated, which is why it was easy for me to want to quit when I got discouraged. I never really felt like it would be possible to realize my dream.

She then gave me the best advice: to break down my reason "why" into achievable goals so I could celebrate small successes on the way to my big dream. I started a separate bank account, which would allow me to put aside a portion of my check each month and do something nice for a family in need. As my checks grew, so did the impact we were able to have on others. We sent a mom's young boys to fine arts camp; we covered medical bills; we built a few ramps for people with physical impairments; we provided holidays to families in need; we traveled to India to help open up orphanages; we were able to give money to many causes that tugged at our hearts. Now I was motivated; now I was being driven by my dreams!

I've heard people in the profession say that your "why" should make you cry. What that means is that your "why" should move you emotionally and keep you enthusiastic about this business during the ups and downs that any entrepreneur can face. It helps you to discipline your disappointments, not to deviate from your mission, and it keeps you driven by your dream!

Everyone has ups and downs, challenges and achievements, disappointments and success. When you are clear about your "reason why," you will continue to be driven by your dream rather than be fueled by your disappointments.

After this chapter, please stop and take the time (I'm talking a few hours) and write down your "reason why." Most people skip over this step, but I can promise you it is the most important. Craft a compelling vision for your future like a movie—as if it were happening in present tense. Don't use wimpy words like, "I wish;" use strong words like "I am." Don't lead with negative phrases like, "I am no longer shy;" make strong, positive proclamations like, "I am confident!" Include the senses and describe your vision: What does your life look like? Your family? Your future? Your home? Your business? Map out all of the people, places, and things that are important to you. Touch on every area of your life. You will know you've accomplished the task when you read it and it motivates and moves you.

When you've completed this, I want you to share it with someone—whether it be your spouse or significant other, supporters in life, or your sponsor in the business. Remember that anything is possible if your "reason why" is big enough!

How do You Eat an Elephant? One Bite at a Time!

Previously I mentioned my "why" wasn't always a motivator because it seemed so far away, so I had to break things down a bit and focus on more bite-sized goals. Equally important to writing your long-term vision or your "why" is setting short-term goals along the way that allow you to celebrate more immediate successes—ultimately paving a path to recognizing your dreams! Successful people always have their next goal in mind.

Goals are dreams with deadlines. Where do you want your business to be this quarter? What titles do you want to achieve? What bonus programs or incentives are you working toward? Write down what they are, when you want to reach them (put it in your planner), and then share them with your sponsor to strategize on the "how." Develop an action plan—what does it take to get there, and whose help will you need? What daily activities will you have to implement yourself and with your team to achieve that goal?

One of my partners and leaders, Carrie, gives great advice. She personally recruited eighteen people her first month in business! She reminds us that what she remembers most is not the eighteen people who joined, but rather the eighty calls she made the weekend that she reached out to those people and set up two full days worth of three-way calls with me, back to back. She coaches her team not to measure "lag measures" (e.g. "I want two new consultants by the end of the month"), but to measure "lead measures" instead (what you can control—your daily activity). Carrie counsels her group to set a daily activity goal as to how many calls you will make a day, how many presentations, and how many sample packs you'll share. Track this. It's even okay to track your "nos." Then you will start to measure the activity it took to meet your target goals, titles, etc.

Create visual reminders by posting pictures of what you're working toward. I have a goal board for all of the things in my life I'm working toward and all of the things I'm praying about. You can even create a constant visual reminder by taking a snapshot of what you're working toward, or who you're working for, and put it on the home screen of your smartphone. Then each time you pick up the phone for a prospecting call and it seems to weigh a thousand pounds, it will motivate you. Paste pictures in your planner so when you look at your planner for your long day's agenda, you are motivated to take action and forge ahead! If you're running for a trip, put a picture of that place where you can see it! If it's a company car, get to a local dealership, take a picture of yourself in that car, and post it so it serves as a daily reminder of what you're working toward. When you visualize something and focus on it daily, it will increase your belief, and it will keep you committed.

One of the keys to achieving a goal is to share it with someone, so I recommend an accountability partner. Choose your spouse, sponsor, or someone in your company who's committed to remaining positive, who's collaborative, and who's working toward something similar as you! Set a weekly talk time to inspire one another, share best practices, and celebrate successes! Social integration is powerful. Processing with positive people allows you to discuss and apply what you're learning! Get an accountability partner right away and start goal setting today! Track your activity daily.

It's up to you to create the vision that inspires action, which ultimately leads to accomplishment for you and your team.

While you're on your journey, play the part. You've heard the old saying, "Fake it 'til you make it." I want to encourage you to play the part of a successful entrepreneur! This includes setting up a professional voicemail on your phone, setting up professional profiles online, and creating professional email signatures that include a link to your website. Get business cards right away! Order brochures or samples from your company to share. Dress the part! You never know when you'll meet your next power player, or where! What do you want people to think of you when they call your phone, receive an email reply, find you on Facebook, or meet you in person? If you want people to believe they can be successful in joining you in your business, you need to play the part. You are an empowered entrepreneur, so let's rock this!

CHAPTER 4

Promoting Products

Ready to ROCK your network marketing business? One of the keys to building a strong, sustainable business is developing a healthy-sized, happy customer base. Why is this so important? Our business is built by the volume that is created by sales to an end customer—whether it is the distributors who are using the products monthly and getting great results, or happy customers who love their benefits! An army full of people on autoship, experiencing incredible results with your product, translates into big business!

There are three ways customer volume is created:

1. Distributors Who Purchase the Product and Become Their Own Best Advertisement

It is highly encouraged that you become a customer of the product by shopping from your own store every month so you can develop your own passion and personal testimonial of the products. If you have a service-based company, use your services. This allows you to come from a place of credibility when promoting your services.

2. Sampling

Always leave your prospects with samples when they attend an event or meeting about the business. This will get them instantly hooked on them and will either build their belief in the business or increase their love for the product so they join you on them even if they decide the business isn't for them. The business isn't for everyone, but the products can be. In fact, I plant the seed during every presentation. I hand them samples saying, "You're going to love our products. If for some reason you decide not to do the business, I'd love to have you as a customer." Remember, I want to gain a consultant (distributor), customer, or connector (referral source) after every meeting. Volume is volume is volume! I want them to join me on the products or the business—either way! If you have a service, is there any way for them to preview it or try it out?

3. Customers Influence Your Volume in a Big Way

A majority of my six-figure per month income comes from the customers who have joined our team! If people are not interested in your business, they can certainly benefit from the products or services your company provides. It's important to nurture this group and encourage them to stick with you as a customer as they account for a good portion of your team volume in the long run. We will talk about how to effectively maintain a happy and loyal customer base in just a bit.

How to Make "Right Now Money"

Customers create a great source of "right now money" and immediate residual income! This volume is extremely helpful to a new distributor in the first few months as they are waiting for duplication to happen and for their organization to build. Customers can also help consultants to qualify and stay qualified for their personal volume goals. Customers also provide great referral sources—not to mention distributors get immediate gratification when people show interest and they immediately get their first check from those customer orders.

If you are in the business and you desire to work part-time building a customer base, that's awesome! You can happily join your company and build some nice residual income on the side for your family! If you want to build a large network and a sizeable income, wealth comes through leverage, and leverage comes from building a team!

Here are my thoughts: I'd rather get paid a percentage on an army full of customers on my team than on 100 percent of just my own sales! Would you rather be the store selling a product, or own the entire franchise? This business model is almost like pseudo-franchising when you build a team! Large organizations are built by a lot of independent business owners each selling a little bit! I could never sell enough products on my own to earn a seven-figure annual residual income—I don't know that many people to sell to!

How do you balance team building and creating a customer base? My mantra is, "Lead with the business and default on the product!" What does this mean? I share the opportunity first with the mindset of recruiting for the company. If they aren't interested, I say something like, "I'd love to have you as my VIP customer," and I share more. I then secure their order and ask for referrals for the business!

I believe creating a sales team sets you up for long-term success. Customer sales create a linear income and if you stop selling or your customers stop purchasing, your income stops, therefore you're always selling. Developing a large organization and focusing on distribution verses sales allows you to develop "walk away income"—an income that grows and is not solely dependent on you. This is the type of income that allows you to someday retire and still get paid! Focusing on creating multiple points of sale rather than getting as many personal sales as possible helps you to do this. Your personal sales will come as a natural result of building an organization. Lead with the business, default on the product!

I do want to give you a little tip: some people get so focused on team development that they forget to offer their product or services. Our team has built a multi-million-dollar monthly organization, but I can only imagine where we'd be today if everyone offered the opportunity for prospects to join them as a customer when they said "no" to the opportunity! Our volume would be even greater! We get paid on volume, and customers are a great source of that volume!

Imagine if your average personal volume or personal consumption base is one hundred dollars per month. You have 1,000 team members, so you get paid on $100,000 volume. Now let's say each of us had an average customer base of $300. Now you're getting paid on a volume of $400,000. We just quadrupled our team volume and our check! Be sure to personally use your product, offer the products to prospects who decide the opportunity isn't for them, gift the products when appropriate, pass out samples, and teach your teams to nurture their customer base! Do the same if you are a service-based company.

How to Get Great Customers

In reality, some people may never be rock star recruiters or desire to recruit in their business, so it's important that you provide a place for these people to plug in and nurture them as they will provide ongoing volume to your growing organization. More than half of my organizational volume comes from happy customers who are purchasing on our team, so it's very important that we discuss how to get customers and how to keep customers happy so they stay with us long-term.

Let's first talk about a few great ways to find customers. Remember to share the business during each of these events, as you never know who may be interested in your opportunity:

1. Host Events in Peoples' Homes

My company isn't a party plan company, but when I started my business, I hosted some events in my home to share the products and the opportunity. I knew if I had limited hours, I would rather spend one hour of my time in front of ten or more people as opposed to talking to one person on the phone for an hour! It was a great way to build my business fast! When I saw the success these events brought, I began calling my friends and family saying, "I have a business that's growing in your area, and I would love to meet new people. Would you be willing to host an event for me? You invite your friends, I will do all the work, and I'll even throw in free product as a 'thank you'!" This expanded my audience,

45

increased my exposure, and helped me to secure more customers and leads for my business.

2. Customer Appreciation Events are Powerful

Once a quarter my local team and I did friends, family, and customer appreciation events. In the evening we would do a "Cocktails and Conversations" event. If it was during the day, we would call them "Coffee and Conversations." Sometimes we would even host a luncheon. We would focus on sharing customer testimonials, highlight new products, do fun games, and drawings. And of course, we mentioned the opportunity and shared our business success stories! Our friends, family, and customers would come and bring their friends! These fun networking-type events would pack the room for us! We always had tremendous results!

3. Gift Your Products at Every Occasion

I am always looking for ways to get our products in peoples' hands, whether it is the holidays, someone's birthday, or as a "thank you." I know if I can get them on the product, they're hooked! Plus it's an open door to a conversation about my business when I follow-up in the future!

4. Social Media and Sharing Stories are a Great Way to Share Your Products

Use your product or service at all times. Make sure your family is, too! Develop a lot of customer testimonials and share them. If applicable to your product, post before-and-afters and testimonials on social media sites.

5. If Your Company Offers Samples, Try Using a Sample Pack Approach

Look for ways to engage in conversation, give someone a compliment, and ask a lot of questions (e.g. "Great service. Do you love your job?" or "Cute kids. Where do they go to school?"). Then leave them with a sample and say, "I've loved chatting with you today. I would love to leave you with this gift [tell them more about the sample, and what it does]. I promise you'll love it. If you promise you'll try it, I promise I'll follow-up!" Get their name, number, tell them what time you'll call, and write it on the card you leave with them. When you follow-up say, "How'd you love the product? Before I tell you more about it, I would love to tell you why I'm excited about my business!" One of our top leaders, Cindy, was prospected this way and is now leading a rockin' team. When she taught our team this approach, it created a huge wave of momentum for us!

Facts Tell, Stories Sell

When talking about your product or service, remember that facts tell, stories sell! Here's a simple outline to follow when packaging your story that you'll share with people you're presenting your product or service to:

1. Share your history or challenge before the products or service.
2. Share how you were introduced to your products or service.
3. Share what product/service you started on.
4. Share the timeframe you saw results (or the immediate results you saw).

5. Then share what "the best part is": share the greatest results you are achieving with your products or service (or hope to achieve).

For example, if you're in skincare you might say, "I really struggled with adult acne and my friend, Robin, introduced me to our acne line. Immediately after I started using it, the swelling went down, the redness decreased, and today I'm so excited to be acne-free!"

Learn to get good at recommending your products and sharing great experiences you've had or others have had. Again, this isn't about sales. It's about sharing when you see someone has a need for what you're offering. It's just like making a recommendation for a good restaurant. When someone shares a problem you can solve, share your story! Once you gain a customer, it's so important to keep them happy. You never know what they'll do (they may join you in the business later, or be a customer for life)! You never know who they'll lead you to through their referrals!

How to Keep Great Customers

How do you keep customers happy? It's important to provide excellent customer service from their enrollment appointment throughout the lifetime of them ordering! Here's what that could look like:

First I recommend you sign up all of your customers on your autoship program that your company offers. Why? This helps you to build steady residual income. It ensures they get the best discounts and benefits.

I walk customers through their first order as I firmly believe good customer service starts on day one. This eliminates the likelihood of order errors or buyer's remorse!

Immediately upon ordering, I send my customers a handwritten thank you card! It's only after shopping at high-end stores that I get a thank you card from a clerk and it always makes a great impression, so I stay loyal to them. A "thank you" is essential! I also go through any necessary instructions with them at the time of ordering.

About a week from the day they place their order, I follow-up with a call. I like to ask questions that will lead on a positive note. I may ask, "How are you loving your experience so far?" This is a good time to be sure they are using things properly and enjoying their experience. If they have any concerns, you can address them immediately.

My next contact is usually a week before their next shipment or billing. When they first place their order, I always note the date on my calendar. This is a great time to make additional suggestions and help them to adjust their order accordingly.

Continual follow-up is key. Be sure to keep your customers in the loop with any exciting product launches, specials, or product-specific events that come to your area, just like some of your favorite stores call you for exclusive shopping events or offers. If you're like me, you usually take them up on it! Treat them like your "VIP" and they will stay loyal to you and committed to the products! Remember, treat them like royalty, and they will give you loyalty!

Customers are a Gift that Keeps on Giving!

I always say happy customers make the best business partners! They are already experiencing incredible results and can be our best evangelists for the company! Don't you think they'd love to monetize that and get a distributor discount, too?

Be sure to follow-up with your customers at some point, saying something like, "How are you loving your results? I'm not sure if I mentioned this, but as a distributor, I get a really great discount on our products, paying wholesale price, and I make money as I share them with others. I didn't know if you'd be interested in hearing more about what we do, but it may be a great way to earn your products for free and some additional income as you send people to your site to order. Would you be interested in learning more? If not for you, you may be able to lead me to someone who this may be great for!"

Lastly, be sure to develop your own "referral rewards" program that rewards customers for referring people on to you for the products or the opportunity. Tell your customers that you're always looking for referrals for your business, and then tell them what you're willing to offer for their referrals—whether it is a small product you can fulfill through your personal order or cash back from your bonus as a "finder's fee."

Don't forget to let your customers know you're expanding in their area. Say something like, "I'm expanding my business in your area and would love to meet more people! Would you be willing to host an event for me? It would just take an hour of your time, you invite people, I'll do the work, and I'm happy to throw in some of your favorite products as a 'thank you.'"

If they host that event, another trick (when people are signing up) is to ask them, "Are these folks coming in under you or under me? Now's your chance to join me!"

Referrals are Rewarding!

Use discretion on how much you're willing to give for referrals of people who end up joining you on the products or the business, or if someone hosts an event for you. Don't forget, referrals can be very rewarding! Some of my strongest distributors came from referral sources! Here are a few examples:

·My personal business partners, Stephanie and Emily, are both top leaders in our company. I met Emily through my sister, Emily. My sister wasn't interested in our business, but I asked her if I could share more with her about what I was doing, in hopes that she could lead me to someone. I further explained there would be referral rewards for her if she did! She agreed, I shared more, and I gave her some ideas of what to email out and a few brief blurbs to post on social media sites. One day, she posted a few sentences online about my business and my story, asking people if they wanted to learn more. A woman at our gym messaged her back, came to one of our meetings, and joined me! Today, Emily's risen to the top of our leader board, has earned more than $10,000 in bonuses with the company on top of her commissions, and also served on our company's advisory board!

How did I meet Stephanie? I used to teach her son in kindergarten! I shared with her what I was doing and she began regularly referring people to me! One day she said, "Why not me?" We met for coffee, and she joined me! Today, she too has earned more than $10,000 in bonuses, has risen to the top of the leader board in our company, and has also earned incredible incentive trips! And the icing on the cake? These two top leaders have become two of my dearest friends.

As you can see, customers and referrals can be very rewarding! Now take what you learned and rock your customer base today!

CHAPTER 5

Power Prospecting

Building a team of rock stars leads to powerful growth and long-term success in the network marketing profession. Power prospecting helps you to find your rock stars.

Talking to people is now what you do for a living, so it must become part of your lifestyle. The more people you talk to, the faster you'll grow, and the farther you'll go in your business. With practice comes confidence. When your confidence increases, so does your set of odds.

I want you to learn to take the pressure off when you're prospecting. Think of it this way: you are just sharing and inviting. You are sifting and sorting. I don't want you to be emotionally connected to the outcome. Think of yourself like a waiter or a waitress pouring a cup of coffee. A server is not offended when you say "no" to the coffee. They keep offering it to everyone. Take all emotions out of it, and if people say "no," keep pouring. Some people say "no" now, but may change their mind later. Always revisit them later. Ask them to be your customer and keep pouring!

As you share with people, keep an open mind. Everyone can plug into your business as what I call one of the three C's:

1. They could be a <u>consultant</u> (distributor) and build the business.

2. They could be a <u>customer</u> and enjoy the products or services you offer.

3. They could be a <u>connector</u>, learn what you do, and connect you to people who may be interested—but they'll only make those connections if they know what you do! Be sure you're sharing with everyone!

A good goal is to reach out to five new people every day—either on your contact list or when you're out and about. You can track contacts on your list by making five checks in your daily planner to chart your progress. You can track new contacts by putting five business cards in your bag with samples—you're done when the cards are gone! You will find your aces if you keep on—trust me! You just have to work through your own set of odds and you won't know what they are until after you've succeeded!

Where do I Find People?

Who can you share your opportunity with? This is the number one question I get from new distributors. The truth is, you are surrounded by people; the question is, are you willing to share with them? Here is a list of a few ways I like to find prospects for my business, along with language to reach out:

1. Revisit Your Customers

"How are you loving your products? I'm not sure if I ever shared, but as a distributor of the products, I get a great discount. I would love to get you on a program where you can get my wholesale pricing too, and possibly earn your products for free or make a little money by sharing them with others. Do you have a few minutes for me to share more?" (Then share your business, distributor discounts and benefits.)

2. Revisit Past Prospects or Former Business Builders When Something is "New"

"I know the timing wasn't right before, but if ever there's a time to take another peek at the company, the time is now. Going into fall and as kids are going back to school, business is booming big time, which will be followed by the boom of the holiday season. Plus, new products and promotions were recently launched. The time is now. I wanted to revisit and see if the time is right to take another look. I would hate for you to miss out." (Share what's new and exciting in your company.)

3. Go Through Your Phone and Facebook Contacts

Is it possible there are people there who you haven't reached out to yet? Call them and say, "I wanted to share some exciting news with you. I started a new business [tell them more about your product or service and your business story, including how you found it and why you're excited about it]. My business is building in your area and I wanted to share it with you to see if I could pick your brain for ideas on how to build there and who you know who might be interested. Could I treat you to coffee [or virtual coffee with a coffee gift card] and tell you more?"

Third party validation and social proof is powerful. After you share more, relate your leader's success story and invite them to hear more from them. You could say something like, "I'm new and still learning. I'd love for you to hear from my business partner. She'll be able to share more and answer your questions." Invite them on a three-way call, to coffee with your sponsor, or to the next meeting or event.

4. Lifestyle Networking

Look for ways to engage in conversation; give someone a compliment; ask a lot of questions: (e.g. "Great service. Do you love your job?" or "Cute kids. Where do they go to school?") Then leave them with a sample and say, "I've loved chatting with you today. I would love to leave you with this gift [tell them more about the sample, and what it does]. I promise you'll love it. If you promise you'll try it, I promise I'll follow-up!" Get their name, number, tell them what time you'll call, and write it on the card you leave with them. When you follow-up say, "How'd you love the product? Before I tell you more about it, I would love to tell you why I'm excited about my business!"

5. Parties/ Virtual Parties

Reach out to your friends and ask them to host an event for you: "My business is building in your area. I'd love to meet new people. Would you be willing to host an event for me? You invite the people, I'll do all the work and throw in some free product as a 'thank you'!" Share the products and your business.

6. Social Media

We are paid storytellers. Mix up your personal and inspirational posts with a little bit of business every few days: lifestyle posts; congratulations and welcoming to new distributors; shout outs to people who made an achievement; encouragement to your team; product tips and testimonials; before and afters; business success stories of people in your company; and anything else to engage and interest your online audience.

7. Networking Groups or Chamber Events

Create strategic business relationships that allow you to meet others so you can help each other grow your businesses. I met one of my top leaders, Stacey, when I set up a booth at a women's networking event in California. She was looking for a home-based opportunity, approached me, and was one of my first leaders in the business. Today she's built to the top of our company and has a large team in the West and beyond!

8. Events

Whether it's a cocktail mixer or a holiday event, when people surround you, it's a great opportunity to collect contact information and connect with them later. Ask them a lot of questions, get to know them better, ask what they do, and when asked about what you do, say, "We're here to enjoy the party tonight, but I would love to tell you more. Let me quickly get your contact information. What's your email? As we expand here in [city], I'm always looking for people to join us. I'll give you a call after [holidays or New Year's] and tell you a little more. You may or may not have a personal interest, but maybe you could lead me to just the right person. I'm looking for referrals."

9. People Who Provide You Services

Think about who you've been supporting for years (hairdresser, nail tech, realtor, etc.). Approach them and say, "I've loved supporting your business for years and now I'm hoping I can share my new business with you. I'd love for you to refer me on!"

How about people who give you great service at a restaurant or store? You can say, "Thank you for your great service. I am looking for people like you for my business. Can we exchange information? I would love to set a time to chat, tell you who I'm looking for, and share more about what I do."

10. Traveling

I love to strike up conversation while traveling. I ask people where they are going and why they are traveling. When people ask where I'm going, I tell them where and say I'm expanding my business there! They typically ask me what I do, which is an open door to share. I always exchange information and follow-up.

11. Creating Your List

Let's take some time on this! Grab a sheet of paper and a pen. I want you to write down every name that comes to mind. Create your contact list of people you know by going through your phone contacts, your Facebook friends, and by reviewing your company memory jogger list. You can also trigger your memory going through old yearbooks, phone books, invitation lists, and even the yellow pages. As you go through each profession A-Z, think about whom you know that's an accountant, a banker, a chiropractor, etc. Your list will be ever growing as you encounter people and think of people, so always keep a notepad and a pen nearby as you continue to grow your list. The larger your list, the more solidly you will establish your business. Network marketing by its very nature requires you to talk to large numbers of people.

I'd like to challenge you to create a list of at least 200 names and think unlimited! I don't want you to think, "Who can I sell to and who can I get to sell this?" I want you to think about who is ambitious, successful, and will want to build financial freedom! Posture is all about knowing what you have—no stress, no overhead, no employees, low investment, huge potential. Where else can people invest less than $1,000 and have the potential to earn a six-or-seven-figure income? Don't beg and don't chase—you are looking for those who are looking for what you have!

Once you've created your list, think like a CEO: Star your top twenty people—your "dream team" candidates. These are the people who, in your wildest dream come true, would join you! Think of the savviest, most well-connected, respected individuals you know—the influencers! These are the types of people that when they pick up the phone, the person on the other line wants to hear what they're doing and be a part of it! These types of people have large centers of influence and tend to build their organizations faster with other people of influence. Do not prejudge them! Here's a good example of why you never judge:

The Story of My $50 Million Mistake

My mom and I used to work for a woman named Stacey. Stacey and her husband own several successful businesses in Chicago. We both thought of her several times and never called her. The chances are, if you think someone is great, someone else does too. Eventually someone will call them, and in this case, they did! Rose out of Chicago beat us to it! She used a referral-based approach, complimenting Stacey and building on her credibility by saying something simple like, "Stacey, I know you've built several successful businesses in Chicago, and I know you're well networked in the Chicagoland area. I respect you. I am building a business in Chicago too. I was wondering if I could treat you to coffee, share with you what I'm doing, and pick your brain for ideas on how to grow this. I'd also like to see if you know people who you think may be interested."

Stacey met Rose for coffee, came with a list of hundreds of names she was ready to give Rose as referrals, and when she heard the opportunity she decided to come to a meeting to hear more for herself. I happened to be hosting the meeting that night and in walked Stacey—my stomach hit the floor! She joined us! Stacey ended up being the top recruiter in the company that year! She just earned her company car, and I have no doubt she will be a million-dollar earner someday too. You heard the story of the "$50 Million Woman" earlier—I guess you could call this my "$50 Million Mistake" considering the substantial sales Stacey's team is creating.

Shoulda woulda coulda? Of course I'm thrilled for Stacey and Rose, but how many know you only have to learn that type of lesson once? Now if someone comes to mind, I follow that little tug in my heart. I have a professional sense of urgency. I call them immediately, and I think, "Which is greater—the risk or the reward?" The worst thing they will say is "no"! You won't die (I have yet to die doing this business)! The best thing they will say is "yes"! And they change your life, their life, and countless other lives too, just as Stacey, Rose, and their upline, Vicky and Prudy, are doing today. By the way, they've created one of the strongest teams in the company!

Don't prejudge anyone. You don't know what their hopes, dreams, desires, or financial situations are. Usually the most well-connected, successful, busy people get it first and they run with it! It's our job to share and it's their job to decide. Remember, if we share what we're doing with everyone, they can all plug in: as a customer, consultant, or to help us in creating new connections! But they can only do that if they know what you're doing and if you share your story with them!

Make this your mantra: "Sharing with five contacts a day keeps leads coming my way!"

Remember to keep your mind and your mouth open—then your business is open! You never know when or where you'll find your next rock star—the whole world is a lead!

CHAPTER 6

Power Presenting

We talked about how to find people to prospect. Now I bet you're wondering what to say next, when you have caught your prospect's attention?

I want to talk for a moment about the power of stories. There's a saying in our profession: "Facts tell, and stories sell." We can share facts and figures about our business until we're blue in the face, but something magical happens when people emotionally connect to our stories and experiences.

When I work with a new distributor on creating their list and discuss who to share their business with, we also work on what to say. I do an exercise where I have them go through their phone, Facebook, and a memory jogger to write down their list of names. I then have them star their top candidates, tell me who they are and why they chose them, and we brainstorm on a way to approach them. One of the most meaningful things we can do when prospecting is share our personal story.

I believe it's really important for you to take the time to work with your team on developing their "business story." Your story about the business is something you can share at meetings, events, your business launch events, and on calls.

Here is a good format to help you create your story:

1. Who are you? (Share your background, a little about yourself, and what you do.)
2. Why were you looking for opportunity?
3. How did you find your business? Why did you join?
4. What results have you seen/ hope to see?
5. What has excited you the most?

Save the best for last: What are you the most excited about accomplishing? Or if you've been in the business, what are your most exciting achievements? Make it meaningful: what will this business do for your family? Here's an example of a business story:

"I was a teacher by trade, looking for extra income as my job stability was really suffering from the economy. My friend, Kris, introduced me to the business. What initially attracted me was the ability to supplement my income, in part-time hours, around the needs of my family and classroom. In very part-time hours I have been able to supplement my teaching income. And with my growing business, I'm on track to match my teaching income by the end of the year. This business is providing me the security that our family needs without having to worry about budget cuts."

When prospects hear you share your story with conviction, they will be moved to want to learn more and find out how it can change their life too. Make sure you smile, exude energy and excitement, and don't use wimpy phrases like, "I hope" or "I wish." Use strong statements like, "With this business we are planning to...." I highly recommend working on your story as you begin making your calls to people on your list. Send it to your sponsor to review. Practice. Then you'll be ready to roll.

Power Prospecting

Let's move right into how you reach out to your prospects by sharing what you're up to and then inviting them to hear more. I'll be sharing with you how to reach out to people you know, people who've been referred to you, and people you meet when you're out and about.

1. Direct Approach

When you go to approach people who are close to you and you're comfortable, be direct! These are usually friends or people you feel really comfortable picking up the phone and sharing just about anything with. For these people I might say something like:

"Hey, Debbie! It's Sarah! I'm so excited to share something with you! Do you have just a minute? Great! I've been dying to tell you about my new business that's expanding in your area—you're one of the first people I thought of sharing this with! Do you have just a few minutes so I can share more?" [Pause.]

Then share your story: how you found your company, why you chose it, and what you're most excited about it doing for you (your business story).

For example: "As you know, I've been facing layoffs teaching and I've always desired to do for my family what I've done for so many others. When I heard how I can start my own business, part-time, around my full-time career, it really got my attention! This will eventually allow me to be able to retire and pursue my passion of becoming a full-time, hands-on mom! I'm so excited!"

"So Debbie, I wanted to share more about what this is and see if you're excited about it too, or if you know anyone who may be. We're looking for partners to join us in business. Do you have a quick minute so I can share more?"

2. Indirect/ Referral Approach

Another approach can be an indirect approach, or a referral-based approach. This may be for someone you know from a professional level, really admire, or may be more of an acquaintance.

For them, your approach may sound something like this: "Hello, Susie. It's Sarah. I'm calling you for a reason today; do you have just a few minutes? I wanted to first start by saying how much I admire you. [Pay them a genuine compliment.] I know you've built an incredible network in Chicago. I'm not sure if I mentioned this, but I am building my business there and I immediately thought of you because I know how well-networked and respected you are there. I'm hoping I can share more about what we're doing and who we're looking to partner with as we expand there, as well as see if this is a good fit for anyone you know in the area. I'd love to pick your brains and get ideas of how to expand my business there. Do you have just a few minutes so I could share more?"

Remember, this is a similar approach to what Rose used with Stacey—seeking her credibility and expertise, and reaching out to her to pick her brain and ask for referrals. Stacey saw the opportunity for herself and joined Rose!

3. Lifestyle Prospecting Approach

What do you say when you're out and about? When striking up a conversation, make it all about the other person. Ask them a lot of questions, almost like you're interviewing them. People love to talk about themselves! Start with compliments, then ask them questions like, "Where do you work?" "Where are you from?" This will lead you into what I like to call your "professional pick-up line" later on. Keep conversing and asking questions, bouncing back and forth like the game of Ping-Pong, and eventually say how nice it was to meet them. Then, go into your professional pick-up line by personalizing the conversation: "Do you have a card?" or "Can I get your email and number?"

"Earlier you mentioned you were from [their city]. My business is expanding to [their city]. I would like to give you a call and take just a few minutes to tell you what we're doing there, who we're looking for, and to pick your brain. I've so enjoyed talking to you—I'd love to reconnect and see if you can help me out."

When asked what you do, share a quick one liner about the company and what you do! Then say, "We just opened this market and the response has been huge. Again, I would love to talk to you about some ideas for expanding the market there and see if you have great connections who would be interested! Can we set up a fifteen minute chat tomorrow?"

4. Sample Pack Approach

If your company offers samples, try using a sample pack approach. Look for ways to engage in conversation, give someone a compliment, and ask a lot of questions (e.g. "Great service. Do you love your job?" or "Cute kids. Where do they go to school?"). Then leave them with a sample and say, "I've loved chatting with you today. I would love to leave you with this gift [tell them more about the sample, and what it does]. I promise you'll love it. If you promise you'll try it, I promise I'll follow-up!" Get their name, number, tell them what time you'll call, and write it on the card you leave with them. When you follow-up say, "How'd you love the product? Before I tell you more about it, I would love to tell you why I'm excited about my business!"

Share, then Invite

When you've reached out to share your story with others, the next step is to invite them to hear more. Your prospect may value a face-to-face chat, and if so, invite them to coffee. Bring along your upline for validation when able.

If there's a live event coming up, those are the most powerful as excitement and energy are high. Typically there are a lot of testimonials shared. Invite them to be your guest of honor, and perhaps you can treat them to a drink afterward to discuss what they've learned?

If you can't meet live, a three-way call with your sponsor or upline leader is very powerful. Simply say, "I want to share more, but I'm new and just getting started. Can I introduce you to my business partner so they can share more with you? This way, you'll get all of your questions answered and this will help me to learn more as well!" (Share your sponsor's success story to provide further validation.) For those of you who are tech savvy, Facetime and Skype are fun ways to have those conversations "face-to-face!"

Power Presenting: Sharing the Story

Once your prospect has agreed to hear more via coffee, call, or an event, what do you say? You have to be able to deliver a quick company story or overview enthusiastically, highlighting the points that appealed to you. Eventually you'll be able to communicate this, tailoring the message to the prospect. Here is some suggested language for a three-way coffee meeting or call to kick it off (and your company will give you messaging tips to tailor the conversation from there):

Fifteen Minute Script for a Three-Way Call or Coffee

C = consultant bringing guest to the call

S = sponsor sharing

G = guest or prospect

C: "Hi, Sarah! This is Kris. I have my friend, Phil, on the line."

S: "Hi, Phil!"

C: "Phil is an incredible businessman and is very well-networked in the metro Detroit area. I told him our business is rapidly expanding there, and I wanted to introduce him to you. Phil, this is my business partner, Sarah, who is going to share more with you about our business that's expanding in your area."

S: "Hi, Phil! Great to talk to you today. I'm thrilled to share more with you. Kris told me great things about you before the call, so I feel like I know you. Before I get started, I'd love to hear what intrigues you most about our opportunity?" [Or, if they know nothing about it yet, have them tell you more about them self.]

G: [Guest shares.]

S: "Thank you for sharing. I'd like to take a few minutes to share our business with you, as well as how and why I got started. Afterward I'd love to hear what questions you have and let you guide the conversation from there. Does that sound ok to you, Phil?"

[Share your packaged story (we taught you how to package that story in the beginning of this chapter). Then, move into sharing more about the company story using an outline I will discuss next called the Five Ps.]

The Five Ps: Talking Points for Presenting

The Five Ps are talking points for you to share your company story in less than five minutes. There is no scripting needed as you should be coming from a place of authenticity!

Get out five notecards, write one of the Ps (listed below) on each card, and write down a few talking points about each one based on your company and product to help you get started! Then practice, but ditch the cards as soon as possible and speak from the heart! By the way, when you share the story, don't talk about the Five Ps with the prospect as that would be strange. Use this as an outline in your head on what to touch on next!

Here they are the Five Ps to talk about when presenting your business:

1. Partnership
Talk about the company you've joined and why it would be great for your prospect. Don't just share features of the company; share benefits to your prospect and why they would be a great fit!

2. Products
Share your own results and the market potential for them (not ingredients).

3. Programs
Share what support they will get from you and the company.

4. Pay Plan
Share how the businesses model works, why network marketing works, and how money is made. I don't share numbers, etc., unless asked. Share how the extra income and incentives could benefit their life.

5. Positioning and Timing
Create urgency as to why the time is now for them to join, such as, "You couldn't have picked a better time to hear about this…. We are now expanding in your market and across the country! I'd love for you to take the lead as we launch in your area!" You can

also create urgency by sharing new product launches or promotions and explaining why the time is *now*!

I'll add in a sixth P: be sure to talk about your prospect's benefits and why this is a great opportunity for them! Help them to dream!

Now back to the script...

S: "With that, we'd love to pass the call back over to you so you can ask any questions you have in regards to the products or how you would get started in the business."

G: [Guest asks questions or makes objections.]

S: [Sponsor answers questions and handles objections, which we will touch on in the next chapter.]

"Based on what I've shared today, what intrigues or excites you the most?" This is a positive, leading question!

G: [Guest gives feedback.]

S: "On a scale from 1-10, how interested are you in what we have to offer?"

G: [Guest gives feedback.]

S: "Do you have a personal interest in learning more about the opportunity or products?" If they don't have an interest, ask, "Do you know anyone who would be interested?"

Next Steps

Based on their interest, use the following systematic approach:

➤ They Have a Personal Interest in Hearing More

Validate why they'd be great, and say, "Here are the next steps: I'm going to send you an informational email. There will be a link to my site to learn more about the products, as well as a link to our opportunity video so you can learn more about the business. I'll also send you a link to one of my business partners sharing her success story, which showcases the possibilities" [send a leader video or story of your choice that may inspire your prospect].

Say, "What I want you to do is go through this information, write down all of the questions you have, and then I'd like to answer those questions on a conference call with my business partner. I have some times free tomorrow and the following day. What time works best?" It's important that you capture the follow-up appointment for the three-way call during that conversation to capture their excitement. The follow-up should be within 24-48 hours. Send them information; set up a three-way follow-up call.

Another option would be to invite them to a local event if they are close by—this can be your business launch, an opportunity meeting, or a big event. It's always powerful when they can see things in person as it builds their excitement.

To review, a proper sequence of exposures is: your first initial contact (which is a casual conversation); send some tools that can do the talking (can be a catalog, bro-chure, a DVD, your website link, or links to company and leader videos); have them review the information and write down questions; invite them to hear more via a live meeting, launch or event, or call; a final three-way call with your sponsor is a great way to answer their questions and bring them to a final decision.

➤ They Have a Personal Interest in the Product

Make a product recommendation for them right then and there, and ask if they have a moment for you to help them place the order. If not, schedule a time for the next day.

➤ They Agree to Provide You with Referrals

Get names, numbers, and ask if they would briefly contact that person to let them know you will be call-ing. Send them an email about the opportunity and ask them to send it to their friends and copy you on it. Tell them about your referral rewards program we discussed previously.

➤ They Have No Interest

Thank them for their time! Add them to your news-letter list and Facebook for monthly follow-up so they become a part of your "audience," watching what you do over time. Again, ask for referrals. If you replace every "no" with a referral, your contact list will never run dry! Follow-up with them from time to time, letting them know what's new and exciting in your company and to see if the time is right to revisit.

The fortune is in the follow-up! After talking to anyone, no matter what the response, I send them a follow-up email thanking them for their time, along with links to our business, products, success stories and my website should they know someone who may be interested or in case they have interest down the road.

You'll always need to be talking to people to keep your business growing. The best way to master the skill is by talking to people every day. As you do this, your skill set increases and so does your set of odds. Practice helps you to rock your presenting skills!

CHAPTER 7

Power Close

Many people are afraid to prospect and present because they fear "not knowing enough" or they doubt their ability to answer questions and handle objections.

I like to answer questions and handle objections by sharing stories of people our prospects can relate to whenever possible. I also like to use the "Feel, Felt, Found Method" so the prospect feels validated. For example, I might say, "I understand how you feel, I felt the same way when I got started, but here's what I found out."

Let me share with you how I'd answer a few common questions and objections:

➤ **"What does it cost to get started?"**
"All of our getting started options are less than [money amount] and you leverage the credibility and resources of our corporation."

Share the kit that allows them the greatest savings and benefits. Then immediately talk down cost objection by sharing any bonus programs or fast starts your company may have in place to help them earn an ROI immediately:

"No matter which starter kit you choose, we have a Fast Start Bonus to help you earn your ROI right away!"

➤ "How does it work? What would I be doing?"

"It's simple. We do two things: promote an award-winning product and a life-changing opportunity. You sell by sharing your results with people you know, people you meet, and those you connect with via social media and networking. We will teach you everything you need to know to be successful. It's simple and super fun!"

➤ "How do I make money?"

I like to give an overview on bonuses, core compensation, and incentives. I keep it simple and quick so it's not overwhelming. If they have more questions, they'll ask.

We get paid through:

1. Upfront Bonuses

Share any bonus programs or fast starts the company offers. Give a general overview: "We have a cash bonus program to help you earn upfront income as well as iPads you can earn the first month."

2. Core Compensation Plan

"We have a great pay plan that allows you to earn on the sales generated by your team. Network marketing is one of the greatest ways to earn residual income (and residual income is hard to find unless you're an athlete with endorsements or a famous singer who gets paid every time his music is played). My team grows exponentially and I am paid on an army full of customers who are elated with their results and are re-ordering throughout the years. I get paid over and over again for work I did upfront. It's one of the smartest business models on the planet!"

3. Incentives

Share your car program or trips offered with the company and say, "We don't just get paid, we get recognized!"

➤ **"I'm so busy. I don't have enough time to do this!"**

"I understand how you feel. I felt the same way when I got started. I was teaching kindergarten full-time and working this business very part-time. But that's not uncommon—we've found that most people work this business in very part-time hours. I started with just about 10-15 hours per week."

Tell stories of people who are working their business part-time and still achieving results!

➤ **"I don't have the money to get started."**

"I can appreciate that. Many people are in the same place because of the recent recession. Because money is tight, this is all the more reason to join us! What if I can teach you a simple way to make the money back with our bonuses during your first month?" If this doesn't work, offer them ideas on how to save up for it!

➤ **"I'm not a salesperson."**

"Terrific! I'm not looking for salespeople! I am not a salesperson either. I'm in the business of sharing our incredible products and the possibility of becoming a turnkey entrepreneur with a global brand! I'm looking for passionate people who, when they love something, share. If I didn't think you could do this, we wouldn't be talking!"

➤ "I don't know anybody."

"What I love about this business is that it's not necessarily who you know, but people you'll meet! Plus, this business is a great way to get to know people. I will teach you exactly how I've found prospects and customers for my business!"

➤ "I don't want to bug my friends or family."

"Thank goodness! I don't want you to bug your friends and family either—that's not what I do! I share what I'm doing and pick their brains to see if there's anyone they know this would be great for. I find out peoples' needs and then I try to fill that need—whether it be a need for my product or a need for extra income. I simply use a referral approach, asking them who they know! Sometimes they identify themselves as being interested in the opportunity! We do that all the time—asking for referrals for babysitters, dry cleaners, etc.!"

➤ "I need to try the products first."

If they are local and I can get a sample packet to them, I say, "Here: try this now and tell me what you think!" Or, tell them their new distributor kit is a great way to sample all of your products, get the best value, and they'll earn as they learn!

➤ "Is this a pyramid?"

First of all, how many times do you think I've heard this? Actually, in my five years of business, I've only heard this objection once because of my belief and posture—both are so strong they're unquestionable. If you're getting this a lot, be sure to connect with one of your leaders about personal and professional development materials that can increase your belief in yourself, your opportunity, and the profession as a whole. If I got this objection, I might say something funny like, "No, why? Is that what you're looking for?"

Or...

"What do you mean by pyramid? Pyramids are illegal. With pyramids there is no exchange of goods or services. We have an amazing product and very loyal customers who are elated with their results! Let's get back to talking about if the business is a good fit for you. What other questions do you have?" I then move on quickly so I don't appear to be on the defense.

"No" Doesn't Mean "No Forever." It May Mean "I Don't Know Enough."

If after answering questions and objections the answer is still "no," don't be discouraged. "No" doesn't mean "No forever," it means "No, not now!" Delay is not denial. So be sure to stay in contact when new products or bonuses launch, or when events are in their area. Say, "I know your timing wasn't right before, but if ever there's a time to take a look at this, the time is now." Some people need multiple exposures and while the timing may not have been right the first time they were exposed, that can change later. I've had people join me a year later! So be sure to follow-up often! Keep them connected to you on Facebook and through your customer newsletters!

And again, don't forget to ask them for referrals, get them on the products, and continue to follow-up!

One of my top leaders, Amy, does this so well. After every prospecting meeting, if they aren't interested, she has a new customer. Eventually that customer becomes a consultant down the road as she's nurtured them, developed a rapport, and has reminded them of the features and benefits of joining her in the business! She's gone on to build one of the top teams on my personal team and has a large base of very happy customers as a result! Remember, the whole world is a lead—*if* you are willing to share!

CHAPTER 8

Power-Start: Effective Enrollment and Duplication

Once you have people joining your team, duplication is where the magic happens. When mastered, you begin to create additional profit centers that create many streams of income in your network marketing business. Duplication begins with effective enrollment, getting your new partner started powerfully, and teaching them how to do the same with their team!

I realize that every leader may have slightly different systems, but the core principles of success in network marketing are the same. Stick with your team's system, and feel free to implement some of the following best practices as you build your team. Core systems include: effective enrollment; connecting your new distributor to company and team tools and training; and then teaching them a sponsorship series that includes creating a list and reaching out to people on their list (and continuing to build it).

Systems are critical. When everyone marches to the beat of his or her own drum, it creates confusion. Why are many of the greatest franchises successful? They have a system they stick to so everyone is doing the same thing. Employees know how to operate. The customer finds comfort in knowing what to expect! Our business model is no different! You have a large group of people with many different backgrounds, so we need to teach them simple actions to take over and over again. It becomes turnkey, just like a franchise!

Effective Enrolling

Let's start at the very beginning—a very good place to start! You've got an excited prospect who's ready to get enrolled! What do you do? I believe good leadership and duplication start at the enrollment appointment. I like to set an enrollment appointment with them where we walk through the application process together, either online or by paper form. I want them to experience the process, and I want to be there to make recommendations and answer their questions. When I sponsor someone, I am making a commitment to help them get off to a great start and to work very closely with them during their first thirty days. I commit to being available for counseling and "income-producing activity" after that (three-way calls, event support, or coaching to help them achieve their next level in business).

When we begin the enrollment process, I ask my new distributor which start-up kit they decided on. This is my opportunity to highlight the features and benefits of the starter packages that contain products for personal use, samples, marketing materials, and training at the greatest savings available. It is my responsibility to share the value. I then enroll them in their monthly autoship and help them get set up with their webpage or website. This is important for *you* to maximize the bonus and commission structures of your company and to ensure *they* easily earn their consultant commissions and have their personal use products conveniently delivered every month.

When they finish their enrollment, I celebrate with them and congratulate them! I then walk them through their personal websites and any company or team training sites that are available to them. I teach them how to enroll a new customer, a new consultant, and where to find all company and team training material that is available to them. I give them the most important "getting started" documents and training so they don't have to dig!

We then dive into a few action items:

1. We discuss their "reason why."
2. We work on their product and business story to share on calls and at events.
3. We discuss immediate goals: What would they like to accomplish the first month? Are there any other immediate bonuses or titles they should be running for based on our company's programs?

I begin their first training sessions within forty-eight hours of enrollment. I focus on two things very heavily their first month:

1. How to create their contact list and begin "exciting" and "inviting."
2. Launching their business with events.

Creating a list and launching their business are two of the most critical activities for a new distributor to see great success immediately.

Creating a List

On the first training call with my new distributor, we begin working on their contact list. We talked about how to create this list in a previous chapter. I walk them through a memory jogger, encouraging them to check the contacts in their phone, Facebook, and any invitation lists they have. I ask them qualifying questions, such as, "Who are the top twenty people on your dream team list? Tell me about them? Why did you choose them?" I then share success stories of people their prospects may be able to relate to so they can share them. We talk about how to approach their top prospects with language and these stories. This gives them the confidence to pick up the phone and also gives them a story to share!

I then walk them through a sponsorship series, which includes:

1. We sit down to make the initial calls to the contacts on their list. If my new consultant isn't local, we block time to do this over the phone. Having me by their side gives them confidence and accountability.

2. They make the initial prospecting call, sharing their story and inviting their prospect to learn more from me: "I'm new and I'm just getting started. I'd love for my partner, Sarah, to share more. Do you have a minute to chat with her? This will also help me to learn a great deal about how to share this, so you'll actually be doing me a great favor!" They then share my success story for validation.

3. Next they make the invitation to next exposure. (If they are local that could be a home business launch or the

next local meeting or event. If they are long distance, they can invite them on a call with me.)

4. Prior to that, they send them information to review (their website, my video, and other company tools provided).

5. Then we have the three-way call or meeting so they can learn more and so we can answer their questions, handle objections, and ask for the order. If they went to a local meeting and do not sign up there, we set up the three-way call to follow. We try to secure them as a consultant/distributor, customer, or connector who agrees to keep their eyes and ears open as referral sources. If they aren't ready to commit and need to research more, we schedule a time to follow-up, send them more resources to review, and invite them to the next exposure.

My goal is to give my new distributor confidence to reach out to those people on their list, share their story and the company story, and teach them to start inviting these people to their events or to three-way calls with me. I teach them about three-way calls, why they are effective, and how to use them.

Daily Activity is the Cure to What Ails You

I then give them daily activity goals. Joe Rubino trains you to use a "3/2/1 Method," which means three prospecting conversations per day, two follow-ups, and one call to a team member to help them take their business to the next level. My mantra is "Five calls a day keep leads coming my way." One of our leaders, Marissa, takes it up a notch and trains her team to use a "5/3/2 Method," which means five contacts per day, three follow-ups with prospects, and two calls to your team members. Considering she began earning a six-figure income in a year alongside her full-time real estate career and young family, I'd say this is great advice. Whatever method, the idea is that daily activity, new activity, and follow-up are where the fortune is.

To track their daily five, they can use a spreadsheet if making calls, or keep track with five cards/samples in their bag if they are going to be out and about networking that day. I want them to set up three calls with me in the next forty-eight hours. Again, we block time to make these calls together. I then set an immediate goal to get their first ten customers on board and their first business partner in that first week. We all know people who would support us if we picked up the phone and said, "I started a new business, and I'm up for my first promotion. I need a few really great orders! Would you be willing to try our award-winning products—you'll get great results, and also help me in getting off to a great start?" Helping your new distributor make their first promotion right away increases their belief, and of course gives both something to celebrate together!

That's a general idea of what I have my new distributor focusing on after their first training: adding to their list; reaching out to the people on it to invite them to learn more; and following up by inviting them to the next exposure. Next I have them look at their calendar and begin thinking about their grand opening launch dates. Then we set our next training appointment and I stay in touch until then, asking them how it's going, who are their hottest prospects, and how I can support them in bringing them on board!

In between the two training appointments, it is my hope they will be reaching out to me to set up three-way calls. Either way, the second training call allows me to follow-up and either talk about how the calls are going, or if they haven't set one up, assess what the issue might be: Are they afraid? Do we need to refine and fix their language? Should we sit down and make the calls together? Are they not reaching people?

Launching Your New Distributor Strong

For your next formal training session, ask them how their contacts are going and who you can help them to bring on board. Then talk a little bit about goals and their grand opening launch events. Open up your calendars and schedule at least three "grand opening" launch events right away (the first within fourteen days). This is a great way to create initial interest and help them to quickly earn their ROI. If they are local, I help and follow the "I Do, We Do, You Do Method" (I do the first one for them while they take notes and learn; the second we do together; and the third they do on their own). If they are long distance, I use Skype video chat to be involved. They hook up their computer to a TV or screen and stream me in live to help present!

Preparation is key to a successful event! I give them ideas on who to invite. I suggest they invite everyone on their list (local or not) as this gives them an excellent lead-in to call their friends and family later to say, "I knew you wouldn't be able to attend my business launch from out of state, but I wanted to be sure to share my new business with you. Do you have a few minutes for me to share more by phone?"

I teach them how to invite. I always recommend they send hard copies of invitations to everyone they know as electronic invites can sometimes get lost. I also suggest they reach out to everyone with a phone call to share their excitement. A personal call of appreciation is very powerful and is a sure way to build a more successful event. I tell them to let their friends and family know about the "grand opening of their business" and how much it means to them that they're there.

These events are typically done at home and the company DVD does the talking while the new consultant, sponsor, and any other consultants there in attendance support the presentation with product and business testimonials. We also focus on a strong close. I teach them how to get orders and appointments set for those interested in hearing more about the opportunity. That's the focus of training topic two.

When you work with a new distributor, your job is to get them off to a fast start, help them earn their ROI immediately, and be by their side that first thirty days. Check in often during those first thirty days by call, text, email, or Facebook to encourage them, remind them of their goals and "reason why," and celebrate their little and big victories! Never forget what it felt like to make your first call, to get your first customer, or to sign up your first consultant!

It is my goal to help them earn a first check they can be proud of, picking up as many bonuses and commissions as possible. Their first check is crucial as it determines whether they stick with you for month two!

I had two "power partners," Marie and Jeannine, promote to the top of our plan in record-breaking time. When they joined me, we got them laser-sharp focused on the first company goal (to earn an iPad). We strategically worked together to get there by working their list and planning events for their local team. We also worked on helping their new partners get off to a fast start! When they reached their first goal, we then looked at the next goal (to earn a company trip) and again, we worked strategically together to achieve that goal. They are now at the top of our pay plan and working toward top tiered incentives. We stayed focused on their goals, locked arms, and matched each other's efforts and pace.

Once your new distributor has learned the system, be sure you stay connected, and always be available for their income-producing activities (which include prospecting meetings and calls) and coaching for as long as they need you! But never do for them what they must do for themselves: keep them plugged in to team meetings and calls; give them ideas on how to continue building their list; connect them with an accountability partner; encourage them to continue to do regular events.

One of my personal partners, Prudy, was a million-dollar earner for another network marketing company. She left her first company to build a medical spa, and came back to our profession to build with our company. She tells a story of when her volume was stagnant and she began to implement ongoing events with her team. She made herself available for all their events as they were income-producing. Within a matter of months she earned the company car and today is one of the top leaders in our company. She works with the willing, focuses on income-producing activity with her team (calls and events), and keeps the rest plugged in!

Staying Connected with Systems

How do you keep your team plugged in when you're working with your new distributors? As soon as you bring someone through the training processes, you need to keep recruiting new people every month so there's always a balance!

I can't stress enough the importance of regular (weekly, bi-monthly, or at least monthly) meetings for your team to stay plugged in. These meetings can be events conducted in your home where your team learns how to "invite" their guests for a presentation on the opportunity, which will then end with some sort of training. Leaders who understand duplication understand the power of regular meetings and events for their team. All a new distributor has to do is learn how to invite a person to a meeting and follow-up after, which makes the process simple and duplicable.

This is how one of our top leaders, Natalia, created a ground-swell in her market. She began implementing regular weekly meetings so her team would duplicate quickly, right out of the starting gates. When she was brand-new, she and her partners would meet weekly in a church, then they grew into a coffee shop, then a restaurant, then a small clubhouse, and then a larger clubhouse. Natalia began earning six-figures within six months, her market became one of the strongest in the company, and now their meetings can attract more than 400 people! She's a million-dollar earner today! She attributes much of that success to having a simple local support system in place where new distributors could easily invite guests, get trained and grow, and this fostered quick duplication and growth! She kept it simple for everyone—how smart!

If your team is long distance, teach them how to establish this system locally. You can host calls and trainings by phone as your team grows. When I began my business, I hosted weekly calls that our entire team plugged into: Sunday nights began with a fifteen minute opportunity call; we took a break for fifteen minutes; then we had a thirty minute training session where different leaders trained on best practices they could implement that week.

Plugging in on a National Level

Regular meetings start small, but they feed into the big national events like "Super Saturday" trainings, leadership summits, and of course, company conventions. Leaders understand the importance of these events and how to promote them (not just announce them) to their team! These big events are like leadership school for our profession! It is where business builders are created. Teachers go to education school, while network marketing professionals attend conventions and big corporate and team events. Leaders never miss an event! These events are where confidence and skill set are built through top training from field leaders and belief is built through outstanding recognition programs and excitement! Minds are made up at these big events—a hobby becomes a career!

When you hear of a big event, take on a leadership role! First sign up yourself (because the speed of the leader is the speed of the team—whatever you do duplicates). Then begin promoting the events to your team! Don't just announce them—share your experience and other leaders' stories of what happened to their business after attending the major events! Tell your team how their business will benefit. You'll notice that major promotions happen before and after these big events because of the excitement and skills that come as a result of attending! What does that mean for you? Bigger growth in your business. Remember, your team goes if you go, and the more people on your team that go, the bigger your check will grow!

Have Fun with This!

You can also create your own fun experiences for your team as it grows! This creates culture, which is the "glue" that holds your team together. The friendships are what keep people in the business when there are distractions in life. Set up parties, barbecues, quarterly recognition events, and team get-togethers at conventions or retreats. A team who plays together, stays together!

As your team grows, so will your leadership. It's important that you decide today what kind of leader you want to be and what kind of culture you create for your team. Always remember, whatever you do will duplicate—starting today!

CHAPTER 9

Preparing Yourself to Lead

Through my experience in network marketing, I've learned a lot about life and leadership. I've made mistakes. I've failed forward. All of the lessons I've learned have refined me and shaped me into the leader I was created to be. My leadership has grown as I have grown up in this profession. Personal and professional growth is one of the greatest gifts the profession has provided me.

As you begin what could be your greatest personal and professional growth journey, I wanted to leave you with a gift and share ten of the top lessons I've learned in my journey to leadership so far!

Ten "Es" to Being an Empowered Entrepreneur!

1. Eighty-six the ego! In this profession there can be a lot of ego. We can also experience a lot of rejection. Humility is the ability to not be moved by flattery or by criticism. Remember that confidence and humility are not in conflict with each other. You can have both at the same time!

   Watch your attitude; never convey a down attitude to your downline (that goes downstream and poisons your group). When you're down, go up! Talk to your upline about your challenges or concerns and let them help you strategize and encourage you! Always be willing to learn, grow, and accept feedback.

Don't compare yourself to others. When we waste valuable energy comparing ourselves to others, we are overlooking our potential and the opportunity for growth in our own life. We might be trying to emulate something someone else is doing, and in the meantime missing our own calling because we aren't doing what we are supposed to be doing! We may have been given a way to do things bigger and better, but perhaps we've missed it as our focus is placed on the wrong things! We are too distracted to notice the gifts in front of us because we are too busy focusing on what others have been gifted with! We have to give that up. Stop struggling, striving, comparing, and competing. The death of contentment is comparison. Competition takes you captive. Focus on your calling.

2. Exude energy and excitement! We are in the promoting business in case you didn't know by now! Meetings, calls, and big events are what catapult people to success. They instill the vision that motives people to join us and provide the excitement that your "volunteer army" needs to forge ahead. Enthusiasm is a catalyst for success! It's important that you exude energy and you learn how to move your team in an authentic way to get to the meetings and attend the big events! That is where belief is built and your teams explode! Don't forget to exude the same amount of energy and excitement every time you do a prospecting call or meeting. Remember, it's the prospect's first time hearing from you, so act like it's your first time giving the presentation. Don't lose that excitement from when you started; excitement is what will create the vision of what is possible for them!

3. Encourage! Good leaders are great at recognition for accomplishments both great and small! I've heard the saying, "People will work harder for praises than raises!" I know that to be true of myself: I once got a handwritten card from our company president and it felt so good to know she was watching what I was doing, and I also wanted to be sure I stayed on her radar. I posted it in my office and it motivated me to take daily action in becoming successful! Recognition can be free, such as a quick call of congratulations to someone on your team who overcame call reluctance, got their first customer or consultant, or made their first promotion! Handwritten notes are powerful! I sometimes like to slip in little five-dollar gift cards to coffee shops and write, "Your business is brewing! Keep it up!" Public praise on social media sites, in a team newsletter, or at a live meeting are not to be underestimated! Be sure to really celebrate major milestones, too! Don't go overboard on expensive items though; it's the thought that counts. When doing recognition, ask yourself: Is this duplicable? (Your team will feel the need to follow your lead with their people.) Is it scalable? (Can you afford it when you have five, fifty, or 500 promotions at the levels you are recognizing?)

4. Engage your team! Good leaders know how to take a spotlight, turn it away from them, and shine it onto their teams. Think of ways you can involve your team at meetings and events. Can you empower people to be greeters or to do setup and takedown? Can you have friendly people serve as greeters? Who can share their success story? Who can you have share best practices or

training tips during training sessions? What about your calls? Can you have a featured success story or another person speak? People "buy in" when they are involved in the process! Engage your team as much as possible!

5. Educate your team! Good leaders take the responsibility to train their teams. They don't rely on anyone else inside or outside the company. When someone commits to the business with you, they are entrusting their success to you! They joined because they believe in you. Keep things simple, teach a system, promote training done by your company leaders and corporation, and be the best leader you can be for your team! If you feel you need support or are no longer committed, direct your team to the leader best capable of supporting them.

6. Equip your team! Develop a mentality that you are out to create empowered entrepreneurs! Turn off your "enabling button." Duplicate yourself as quickly as possible. Don't get stuck in "management mode" thinking you should or have to do everything yourself. Encourage your team to rise to the challenge and develop their own leadership right away!

7. Encouragement is important! Good leaders know how to elevate and lift up the entire organization, which includes their corporate team, upline, downline, and the sideline sisters and brothers not on their team. Why is it important to encourage your company? So your team feels a sense of security in who they're entrusting their future to. Why elevate and lift up your downline? I think that's an obvious as they contribute to your income and

they will either appreciate or resent that based on their relationship with you. Why encourage your upline? This is critical for them to be effective when working with your team on calls and at events. Use your words to build up, not tear down. It all comes back to you. How you speak of others is a true reflection on you. Make integrity of the utmost importance as your character is the only thing that follows you.

8. Ethical leaders go the distance! Be a person of abundance and integrity: do the right thing at all times, tell the truth, honor your team and the company, and don't gossip. I love how my friend, Orrin Woodward, leads. When someone comes to him with gossip, he asks, "Can I go to that other person right now and quote you?" If the answer is "no," he knows they aren't looking for solutions, but rather to gossip. He has created a culture of excellence with his group, and when there's conflict, the goal is to find resolution.

Treat the prospects of others with respect. If they come to a meeting and the sponsor is not there, tell them, "You're in great hands with Susie Q," and treat them kindly, immediately connecting them back to the person who shared the opportunity with them! There will come a time when you'll want someone to do that for you. How you interact with the distributors in the company will be what you see duplicate down on your team.

9. Lead by example! Whatever you do duplicates, so don't train on things you're unwilling to do, set the pace for your team, and never stop recruiting and building. If

you stop building before you have a solid income and title, you will fail in this business. No one can truly succeed sponsoring a few people a year. New blood brings life to the business. Stop recruiting and you die a slow death in network marketing. Your business will come to life again when you recruit!

Remember to work with the willing and love the rest of them. Work with those who deserve your support (not necessarily those who need it). How do you identify those who deserve it? By their actions! I recently heard a leader say, "I watch their feet, not their mouths!" In other words, watch what they are doing, not what they are saying they are going to do. Match your team's efforts!

10. Endure, endure, endure! Pick a company and stick with it. The grass is never greener on the other side; the grass is only green where you water it! Never forget my friend, Susie's, story—you never know what people will do or who they'll lead you to. Her sponsor quit and made a $50 million mistake! You are just working through your own set of odds and you will find your aces if you don't quit.

There will be ups and downs on your journey. Success requires you to fail forward. Discipline your disappointments, don't deviate from your mission, and be driven by your dream. Don't quit.

You can either give up when times are tough, assuming your business isn't working for you, or you can continue to learn your own life and leadership lessons as you move ahead. You'll eventually find success as long as you don't quit and continue working!

CHAPTER 10

Power of Belief

My husband and I recently went to India with friends to open up orphanages. It was a life-changing experience. One of the greatest memories of my lifetime was when my husband, Phil, and I witnessed fifty children run into their new home like they were running into Disney World. Their smiles sparkled as they lay on their brand-new beds for the very first time. We wrapped our arms around the children and welcomed them into more than just their new homes, but their brand-new lives. We played with them, taught them games, sang with them, and loved on them. Many times we remarked how if it weren't for our network marketing business, we would never have had that experience. There is no way we could have taken weeks away from our jobs. We couldn't have even afforded the immunizations—let alone travel expenses—before our network marketing business.

It takes time and money to pursue many of our life passions. Network marketing can be the greatest vehicle to provide the time-freedom and financial-freedom necessary to live a life you love. Your dreams, desires, and passions were placed in your heart for a reason, and I don't believe there's a dream or desire in our heart that cannot be fulfilled. It doesn't matter where you are now in your business, your dreams can be realized through this vehicle. You just have to remain coachable and committed; you can never give up.

As I write this, I just celebrated the success of one of my leaders, Nikki. Just two days ago, she was promoted within our company to the top of the pay plan. In the past few months, her team tripled their volume, she is on track to earn a company car by the end of the year, and she is pursuing her dream of working with children in need around the globe through the resources her network marketing business has provided her.

Here is what I love most about Nikki's story: She's been in the business for almost three years and she only started seeing notable success in our business in the past few months. Most people would've given up much sooner. She admits that there were many times she wanted to quit, wondering if success would ever happen for her. Although discouraged at times, she continued to remain coachable and committed. I would speak words of affirmation to her, reminding her of her dreams, and how much I believed in her.

I spoke to Nikki about the power of her words and encouraged her to declare greatness over her life, business, and her team. Nikki began to speak faith-filled words even when success didn't seem possible.

During this time in her business, Nikki's faith was being built, her confidence was being built, and she was being refined into the leader and woman she was intended to be. Over the past ninety days, her business was completely transformed, and now I can barely recognize Nikki! She has become a dynamic, strong, assured leader.

Nikki's story was recently shared on a national call with my team, and it inspired so many to press on, persevere, and to push toward their prize. I encourage you to also persevere. You will face resistance in your business, too. There might be times when you want to quit. Resistance isn't a sign to quit. You are exactly where you are supposed to be—growing in faith, confidence, and as a leader. You are being refined. You will be accelerated at your designated time if you press on.

What do you believe for your business? What do you believe for your life? What are you speaking over your business, life, and team?

You have the ability to speak into someone's destiny! Just as I spoke into Nikki's life, and she in turn spoke into her team, you have the ability to truly transform lives with your words. We give life to what we say, good or bad.

Remember me sharing how I wanted to quit so many times? Today I am the top earner of our company, but when I began I used to be one of the lowest earning leaders. My company president jokes how I quit more times than anyone else in our company. I used to say, "I'm young. All of my friends are young. No one is joining me." Then when people were joining me I would say, "Everyone is quitting!" I was definitely in a holding pattern myself, but looking back, I realized I was exactly where I needed to be. I wasn't ready to lead yet—I was being refined into the leader and woman I was destined to be, being prepared to lead the multitudes.

We all have impact on lives—whether it is in our marriage, our ministry, our families, our business, or our career. We all have people who are depending on us to be effective and to cast a vision for them to reach their full potential in life. I used to have great impact on little lives as a teacher, and now we have influence over many adults in our business, as well many little lives around the globe.

When our feet were planted in that first orphanage in India, Phil and I looked at each other with tears in our eyes and said, "It was all worth it." All the hard work, tears, rejection, and "nos" over the past five years were worth it. We know our visit to India wasn't the end for us, but rather the beginning. This one experience transformed our lives. Our purpose and plan for our life unfolded right before our eyes. It was beautiful to see our reason "why" in action.

Network marketing has fulfilled our dreams, as well as fulfilled the dreams of those we share our business with and the children around the world who we bless with the resources and time it's providing us.

Don't give up on your dreams—ever! And remember, it's never too early or too late to passionately pursue your dreams! Go for your gold!

Now's your time! Get ready to shine!

Rock on, rock stars,
Sarah "Rockin'" Robbins

ABOUT THE AUTHOR

Sarah Robbins is a kindergarten teacher turned seven-figure annual residual income earner in network marketing, and is considered one of the world's leading network marketing consultants. Now in the top 1 percent income bracket of all women in America, she began part-time with no business experience and by the age of twenty-nine, had achieved a six-figure per *month* income within her network marketing company. Sarah has been featured in many best-selling network marketing books and is a frequent speaker at top industry events. As a speaker, she contributes unique insights on success, prosperity, leadership, and network marketing topics, and is fulfilling her lifelong dream of helping others.

Grow Your Business!
You can receive Sarah's
FREE VIDEO for MLM success at:
www.SarahRobbins.com/free-video

DISCOVER SARAH ROBBINS'
SEVEN-FIGURE SUCCESS SYSTEM!

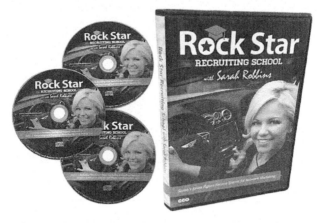

Rock Star Recruiting School with Sarah Robbins:
Seven-Figure Success System for Network Marketing

Welcome to the Rock Star Recruiting School! For this series, Sarah is inviting you "back to school" in your network marketing business.

You'll discover how to develop an entrepreneur's mindset, build bigger volume with a large customer and consultant base, master the art of inviting, give powerful presentations, establish simple systems for dynamic duplication, and much more!

- Session 1: Preface: Building Your Belief in the Profession
- Session 2: Preparation: Developing Your Blueprint for Success
- Session 3: Products: Getting and Keeping Customers
- Session 4: Prospecting and Presenting: Mastering the Art of Inviting
- Session 5: Perfecting "The Close": Three-Way Calling and Handling Objections
- Session 6: Power Start: Effective Enrollment, and Duplication

Available at: www.SarahRobbins.com/store

CONNECT WITH SARAH ROBBINS

www.SarahRobbins.com

facebook.

www.Facebook.com/sarahrobbinsfanpage

twitter

www.Twitter.com/sarahrobbins1

www.YouTube.com/skincareconsultants

www.Linkedin.com/in/sarahrobbins1